# JOINT AND DOUBLE DEGREE PROGRAMS: AN EMERGING MODEL FOR TRANSATLANTIC EXCHANGE

# JOINT AND DOUBLE DEGREE PROGRAMS: AN EMERGING MODEL FOR TRANSATLANTIC EXCHANGE

EDITED BY DANIEL OBST AND MATTHIAS KUDER

*This book is part of a policy project funded by the EU-U.S. Atlantis Program of the U.S. Department of Education's Fund for the Improvement of Postsecondary Education (FIPSE) and the European Commission's Directorate General for Education and Culture.*

New York

IIE publications can be purchased at: www.iiebooks.org

Institute of International Education
809 United Nations Plaza, New York, New York 10017

© 2009 by the Institute of International Education
All rights reserved. Published 2009
Printed in the United States of America
ISBN-13: 978-0-87206-318-1
ISBN-10: 0-87206-318-6


Library of Congress Cataloging-in-Publication Data

Joint and double degree programs : an emerging model for transatlantic exchange /
edited by Daniel Obst and Matthias Kuder.
      p. cm.
   Includes bibliographical references.
   ISBN 978-0-87206-318-1
   1. Joint academic degree programs. 2.  University cooperation.  I. Obst, Daniel. II. Kuder, Matthias.
   LB2381.J65 2009
   378.2--dc22
                              2009034984

# TABLE OF CONTENTS

## Putting Programs into Practice

## Sustainability – Building Networks to Support Continued Programming

## Program Profiles – Overviews of Selected Transatlantic Degree Programs

## The European Experience – Program Design and Implementation

## Appendixes

Managing editor: Shepherd Laughlin, IIE

Cover and text design: Pat Scully Design

# FOREWORDS

BY ALLAN E. GOODMAN, PRESIDENT AND CEO
INSTITUTE OF INTERNATIONAL EDUCATION

Joint and dual degree programs are quickly gaining attention in the U.S. as ways to offer particularly deep and meaningful international experiences to college and university students. While joint and dual degree programs are often complex to implement, they also provide a chance to build particularly strong institutional partnerships between U.S. and European higher education institutions, and they are an important element of the transatlantic educational exchange relationship.

Since the Institute's founding in 1919, IIE has been dedicated to promoting academic exchange between the United States and Europe. Some of IIE's earliest work involved coordinating exchanges with European governments. Later, in the 1930s, IIE's first Assistant Director Edward R. Murrow helped European scholars relocate to the U.S. and lecture or research at U.S. colleges and universities. After World War II, the Institute arranged for more than 4,000 U.S. students to study and work on reconstruction projects at European universities.

This strong relationship continues today and continues to be reflected in the work of IIE. The Fulbright Program, which IIE has been honored to administer on behalf of the U.S. Department of State since the program's inception, regularly sends students to over 40 European and Eurasian countries, and the region hosts more U.S. Fulbright students than any other. The Fulbright Scholar Program, administered by CIES, a division of IIE, sent 354 scholars to Europe and hosted 367 scholars from Europe during academic year 2008/09. Since 1990, IIE has operated a regional office in Budapest and administered a range of scholarship and fellowship programs throughout the region. In recent years, dozens of European institutions have joined IIENetwork, IIE's institutional membership program.

Our commitment to the region is part of a recognition that with the largest bilateral trade and investment relationship in the world, the EU and the U.S. will only be able to solve common challenges through the kind of mutual understanding and intercultural cooperation created by transatlantic exchanges.

Transatlantic joint and dual degree programs are an exciting new dimension of the longstanding exchange relationship with Europe and of IIE's commitment to expanding the number and diversity of American students who study abroad. We thank the U.S. Department of Education's Fund for the Improvement of Postsecondary Education (FIPSE) and the European Commission for supporting our efforts to make more information about these programs available.

BY DIETER LENZEN, PRESIDENT
FREIE UNIVERSITÄT BERLIN

Today, higher education institutions face manifold challenges. Hardly any university is unaffected by global developments, whether the current economic downturn or the increasing competition for the best brains and most talented students. However, we at Freie Universität Berlin strongly believe that challenges also hold opportunities. We are convinced that deepening our international partnerships and broadening our global networks are the way forward.

This rationale manifests itself in the International Network University strategy that we have adopted for Freie Universität. It is based on the reasoning that excellent research and teaching is neither one-dimensional nor bound to national borders, that cooperation across disciplines and across borders is the only way in which academia can successfully address the various challenges of our century, and that as a university, we have the obligation to provide our students with the knowledge and skills needed to succeed in an increasingly globalizing world.

As one of nine German Universities of Excellence, we continue our commitment to build reliable and inspiring frameworks for students, faculty, and administrators based on the idea of curriculum cooperation, structured exchanges, shared supervision of doctoral students, and collaborative research. A joint PhD program with renowned Mexican universities focusing on "Movements, Actors, and Representations of Globalization" and a joint master's program in journalism with the Lomonosov Moscow State University are but two recent examples of this commitment.

Deeply rooted in transatlantic tradition, Freie Universität Berlin takes leadership in promoting dialogue and cooperation between Europe and North America. We are delighted to work with the Institute of International Education, our other partners and the authors of these articles to inform discussion about collaborative degree programs. We trust that this publication will be a valuable source of information for higher education institutions on both sides of the Atlantic and beyond.

# Introduction

By Daniel Obst and Matthias Kuder

Cooperation in higher education between the United States and Europe has been based to a great extent on traditional student and faculty exchange programs. These have over decades enabled many students to experience living and learning on the other side of the Atlantic, thus creating important institutional linkages and a profound understanding of the respective countries and cultures.

In recent years, developments on both sides of the Atlantic have created new opportunities for transatlantic collaboration in higher education. One of the more prominent recent developments involves the emergence of collaborative degree programs, such as dual diplomas, joint degrees, consortia, and other forms of curriculum cooperation arrangements. Among European countries joint and double degree programs have long been a vital part of internationalization strategies in higher education, helping to create stronger links and flourishing institutional partnerships, as well as preparing students for a global workplace. In the North American context, such programs have been until recently a less common feature of internationalization strategies. However, the interest in curriculum cooperation is gaining momentum not only in the U.S. but in most countries around the world. In an increasingly global and competitive higher education market, collaborative programs can offer a distinct set of advantages and are an important asset in the struggle for attracting the best and the brightest.

The emergence of these types of deep institutional linkages and the discussions among educators and policymakers in Europe and the U.S. on the value of joint and double degree programs have to a certain extent been precipitated by the changes in the higher education system in Europe, including the Bologna Process. The variation in the duration of bachelor's degrees has especially been at the core of discussions between European and U.S. universities. With the establishment of bachelor's and master's degrees in Europe, many traditional exchange agreements between European and U.S. universities will have to be retooled.

Though the Erasmus and Erasmus Mundus programs have enjoyed incredible success in promoting student exchange within and into Europe, some signs indicate that European students have been less likely to study in the U.S. in recent years. According to the most recent statistics from the Institute of International Education's *Open Doors Report on International Educational Exchange*, the number of students from the European Union studying in the U.S. has declined by 10% since 2001/02—a trend that has international education professionals worried on both side of Atlantic. Declines from key European sending countries are particularly worrying: students from Germany, the leading sending country from Europe to the U.S., have dropped 7% since 2001/02.

Another challenge to transatlantic academic exchange is the increasing predominance of short-term study abroad programs in the U.S. While Europe remains the leading destination for U.S. students who study abroad, the length of study abroad sojourns has declined dramatically in the past decade. Currently, only 6% of all U.S. students who study abroad spend a full academic year in the host country, according to IIE's *Open Doors* report. The majority of study abroad programs are short-term programs of eight weeks or less, which may have less of an impact on the development of intercultural skills and foreign language abilities. Medium-term and long-term study abroad sojourns, especially if conducted in a structured way in cooperation with local partner institutions and including exposure to local students and faculty, may hold far greater opportunities in this respect.

In order to address these concerns, colleges and universities are beginning to explore new methods of transatlantic academic cooperation, including increased curricular integration, more bilateral partnerships, twinning, and consortia. In the context of the two-cycle degree structure in Europe, the development of joint and double degree programs between European and U.S. higher education institutions, both at the undergraduate and graduate levels, is particularly appealing because of the profound impact these programs have on the institutions involved. On the other hand, joint and double degree programs may only have limited impact on the total number of students exchanged across the Atlantic.

So far, little research exists to inform institutions in Europe and the U.S. on the context in which these programs operate. Similarly, there have been few opportunities for higher education institutions, particularly U.S. institutions, to engage in dialogue on successful models of curriculum cooperation with foreign countries. One exception in this regard is the EU-U.S. Atlantis Program, which is supported by the U.S. Department of Education's Fund for the Improvement of Postsecondary Education (FIPSE) and the European Commission's Directorate General for Education and Culture. Not only has it contributed to the establishment of numerous transatlantic degree programs through the funding it provides, but its annual grantee meetings have also emerged over time as a central platform for discussing the development and successful implementation of joint and double degree programs. One other notable example is the Transatlantic Degree Programs (TDP) project, an initiative by the Freie Universität Berlin and the German Academic Exchange Service (DAAD), which over a period of three years offered a series of expert workshops in Europe and North America with the aim of facilitating knowledge transfer and best practice examples in cross-border curriculum cooperation.

The goals of this publication are to expand the knowledge about existing transatlantic degree programs and to address the challenges and opportunities in developing joint and double degree programs—especially in the transatlantic context.

The articles in this book are divided into six thematic sections. The first section, which focuses on the theories behind transatlantic degree programs, examines the key findings of an extensive survey conducted in spring 2008, based on responses from 180 higher education institutions in the U.S. and the European Union. The chapter addresses the current landscape of transatlantic degree programs and identifies inherent challenges and opportunities of expanding existing or developing new programs. Pascal Delisle analyzes the rationales and strategies behind joint or double degrees and sheds light on why universities enter into such close collaboration. Stephan Geifes points to the motivations behind the renewed interest in transatlantic degree programs in the past few years.

The second section of this book focuses specifically on communications and securing institutional support, a process that provides the foundation for any joint program. Allan Lerner and Nora Bonnin address the role of policy, procedural and financial considerations in securing institutional support, while Jerome L. Neuner discusses ways to create clear channels of communication, both within the home institution and with partner institutions. Lori Thompson discusses the State University of New York's approach to curriculum design and communication in dual diploma programs, and Ulla Kriebernegg and Roberta Maierhofer discuss issues of curriculum design raised while setting up a program at the University of Graz.

The third section, "Putting Programs into Practice," presents four perspectives on the beginning stages of a joint or double degree program. Macarena Sáez and Jamie Welling look specifically at programs in law, and Régine Lambrech discusses an engineering program. Vuokko Iinatti and Tuija Mainela describe the particular challenges involved in student selection for such intensive programs, and Kathleen E. Murphy and Paul Tomkins suggest a new joint ownership model for the administration of joint degrees.

Sustainability is a key question in any joint or double degree program and is the subject of the fourth section of this book. Jeffrey W. Steagall, Jeffrey Michelman, and Anne Sheridan Fugard explore how institutional relationships permit sustainability over time, and Sarah A. Hutchison discusses the contribution of alumni networks to sustaining a programmatic identity.

The last two sections consist of articles focusing primarily on specific joint and double degree programs. First we present "program profiles"—broad views of selected transatlantic programs. El Nault presents an overview of a transatlantic program for economics students, and Peter Gustavsson and Emeric Solymossy discuss "value creation" and how it relates to their transatlantic degree program. John E. Pakkala, Jürgen E. Blechschmidt, Joseph C. Musto, and Hans H. Reddemann describe a collaborative program for mechanical engineering students between a U.S. and a German institution. Finally, Jenifer S. Cushman describes a degree program offered by a small college in Pennsylvania and a German University of Applied Sciences.

The final section consists of two articles that review lessons learned from joint and dual degree programs in the European context. Carsten Klenner and Christi Degen use the Double Master in Business Administration at the University of Cologne to take a close look at issues of credit transfer. Hilary Jones and Christopher Grinbergs describe their experience managing a joint program at Roehampton University.

Throughout the publication, the authors refer to collaborative degrees in a number of ways, including *transatlantic, joint, double, dual,* etc. In general, a multitude of meanings can be assigned to these terms on both sides of the Atlantic. Often enough, and this is particularly true for the U.S., these terms may refer to programs that combine degrees in two academic disciplines yet are carried out entirely within one and the same higher education institution. Also, there is frequent confusion about the difference between the terms dual and double. While in some countries the term *dual degree* is used more commonly for degree programs that feature structured curriculum cooperation with a foreign partner institution, elsewhere *double degree* might be the predominant term to describe such jointly offered academic programs.

The rapid increase of collaborative programs on both sides of the Atlantic and beyond is likely to further accelerate the variation in terminology and formats of collaborative degrees. Naturally, such developments prompt questions about legal aspects, quality assurance and accreditation issues. In the absence of internationally binding standards—and control thereof—individual examples of malpractice in the field of joint and double degree programs might tarnish the image of cross-border curriculum cooperation making efforts to define a common terminology for collaborative programs especially important.

Terminology in this book varies slightly, but the most common definition of what constitutes an (international) *joint/dual/double* degree used here is:

A joint degree program: students study at (at least) two higher education institutions and receive upon completion of the study program a single degree certificate issued and signed by all the participating institutions jointly.

A dual or double degree program: students study at (at least) two higher education institutions and receive upon completion of the study program a separate degree certificate from each of the participating institutions.

This book is part of a policy project, the Transatlantic Degree Programs (TDP) Inventory Project, that is funded by the EU-U.S. Atlantis Program. The Consortium members include Ursula Lehmkuhl and Matthias Kuder at the Freie Universität Berlin, Stephan Geifes, formerly at the Franco-German University (DFH) and now Scientific Coordinator at Deutsches Historisches Institut in Paris, Andrejs Rauhvargers of the Latvian Rectors' Council, Daniel Obst at IIE, and Robert Gosende and Linda Veraska at the State University of New York (SUNY).

In addition to the project partners, we wish to thank several individuals and institutions who have been instrumental in shaping this project and without whom this project would not have been possible: Diego Sammaritano at the European Commission and Frank Frankfort and Ralph Hines at FIPSE for ongoing advice and support.

Britta Baron of the University of Alberta has been a major source of inspiration and expertise for this initiative from its very onset and has provided invaluable advice throughout the duration of the project. We are also grateful for the support and advice of the German Academic Exchange Service (DAAD).

Special thanks go to Shepherd Laughlin, Program Coordinator at IIE and managing editor of this book, for his invaluable support.

Finally, thanks go to all the authors who have contributed these excellent chapters, which help raise awareness of the challenges and opportunities inherent in conceiving, implementing and sustaining joint or double degree programs in the transatlantic context.

# JOINT AND DOUBLE DEGREE PROGRAMS IN THE TRANSATLANTIC CONTEXT: A SURVEY REPORT

DANIEL OBST AND MATTHIAS KUDER

This article, based on a report published by the Institute of International Education (IIE) and Freie Universität Berlin in January 2009, seeks to describe the features of existing transatlantic degree programs and to address the challenges and opportunities in developing joint or double degree programs – especially in the transatlantic context. This article examines responses from 180 higher education institutions in the United States and the European Union to an extensive survey conducted in spring 2008. The survey was part of a project funded by EU-U.S. Atlantis Program of the U.S. Department of Education's Fund for the Improvement of Postsecondary Education (FIPSE) and the European Commission, and was launched in cooperation with several leading U.S. and European institutions: the Institute of International Education and State University of New York (in the U.S.), and Freie Universität Berlin, the Franco-German University, and the Latvian Rectors' Council (in the EU). The major goals of the survey were to assess the current landscape of transatlantic degree programs and identify inherent challenges and opportunities of expanding existing or developing new programs.

The survey was conducted from March 24 to June 27, 2008. Higher education institutions on both sides of the Atlantic were invited to participate in the web-based survey. The survey received valid responses from 180 higher education institutions in the European Union, the United States, and other non-EU countries in Europe. Fifty-one percent (92) of the respondents represented EU institutions, 45 percent (81) represented U.S. institutions, and 4 percent (7) represented non-EU countries. Because so few responses were received from non-EU countries, these results have not been considered in the analysis that follows. References to "European" refer to EU institutions. Most survey respondents were senior administrators within their institutions or departments and included 15 deans, 66 directors or heads, and more than 30 other senior administrators such as vice provosts, associate provosts, and associate deans.

## Number and Type of Transnational Degrees

Double degrees appear to be much more common than joint degrees. Among the survey respondents, 13 percent of U.S. institutions offer joint degrees while 68 percent offer double degrees (Table 1). On the European side, 26 percent of institutions offer joint degrees, and 76 percent offer double degrees. EU institutions are about twice as likely to offer at least one joint degree as U.S. institutions and somewhat more likely to offer at least one double degree. Although the percentage of EU and U.S. institutions offering at least one double degree is similar, EU institutions are likely to offer about twice as many such degrees as U.S. institutions. U.S. institutions were more likely to offer joint and double degrees at the undergraduate level, whereas EU institutions were much more likely to offer such degrees at the graduate level and above (Table 2).

TABLE 1: PERCENTAGE AND NUMBER OF COLLABORATIVE DEGREE PROGRAMS AS REPORTED BY RESPONDING INSTITUTIONS

|  | Percentage | | Total # | |
|---|---|---|---|---|
|  | U.S. | EU | U.S. | EU |
| Joint Degrees | 13 | 26 | 38 | 50 |
| Double Degrees | 68 | 76 | 240 | 613 |
| Joint and/or Dual Degrees in Planning Stage | 87 | 85 | 110 | 172 |

Source: Transatlantic Degree Programs Survey 2008

TABLE 2: TOTAL NUMBER OF JOINT OR DOUBLE DEGREE PROGRAMS CURRENTLY OFFERED BY RESPONDING INSTITUTIONS, BY ACADEMIC LEVEL

| U.S. Institutions: | | | | |
|---|---|---|---|---|
|  | Undergraduate | Graduate | Doctoral | Other |
| Mean | 2.3 | 1.7 | 0.2 | 0.3 |
| Median | 1 | 1 | 0 | 0 |
| Total # of Programs | 149 | 115 | 10 | 17 |
| **EU Institutions:** | | | | |
|  | Undergraduate | Graduate | Doctoral | Other |
| Mean | 1.4 | 6.2 | 1.4 | < 0.1 |
| Median | 0 | 2 | 0 | 0 |
| Total # of Programs | 126 | 548 | 127 | 4 |

Source: Transatlantic Degree Programs Survey 2008

## Partner Regions and Countries

Both European and U.S. universities were more likely to have joint and double degree programs with European partner institutions than with institutions in any other region. Among EU institutions, 86 percent had programs with other EU institutions while 53 percent of U.S. institutions had programs with EU institutions. Very few joint or double degree programs were reported with the Middle East and Africa.

FIGURE 1: PERCENTAGE OF RESPONDING INSTITUTIONS THAT HAVE ESTABLISHED JOINT OR DOUBLE DEGREE PROGRAMS WITH INSTITUTIONS IN SPECIFIED COUNTRIES AND WORLD REGIONS

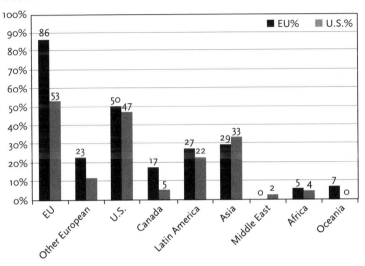

Source: Transatlantic Degree Programs Survey 2008

The top five countries where EU respondents had established joint and double degree programs were all in Europe, with the exception of the United States. The top partner country for European respondents was the United States, followed by France, Spain, Germany, and the UK. The top partner country for U.S. institutions was Germany, followed by China, France, Mexico, South Korea, and Spain. While European countries also figured prominently in the responses of U.S. institutions, many reported having developed joint or double degree programs with institutions outside Western Europe—in China, South Korea, Mexico, and Turkey.

## FIGURE 2: Most frequently cited Foreign partner countries

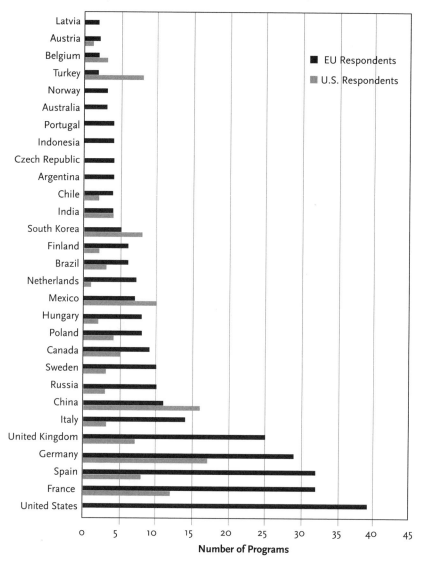

*Other countries listed by EU institutions: Albania, Colombia, Denmark, Estonia, Greece, Ireland, Japan, Malaysia, Peru, Romania, Singapore, Slovenia, South Africa, Suriname, Switzerland, Tanzania, Thailand, Vietnam.*

*Other countries listed by U.S. institutions: Bahamas, Bolivia, Colombia, Dominican Republic, Ecuador, Ghana, Honduras, Ireland, Japan, Kuwait, Peru, Singapore, South Africa, Sri Lanka, Switzerland.*

Source: Transatlantic Degree Programs Survey 2008

## Academic Disciplines

About half of the responding U.S. and European institutions report offering joint and double degrees in the field of business and management, making this by far the most common field of study for these degrees. The second most common academic discipline was engineering, with 29 percent of EU institutions offering joint and double degrees in the field, compared to 21 percent of U.S. institutions. U.S. institutions were slightly more likely than EU institutions to offer these degrees in most other fields, such as social sciences (16 percent U.S., 11 percent EU) and communications (9 percent U.S., 4 percent EU). One exception was law, a field in which 8 percent of EU institutions offered a joint or double degree versus 2 percent of U.S. institutions.

FIGURE 3: TOP ACADEMIC DISCIPLINES IN WHICH JOINT OR DOUBLE DEGREE PROGRAMS ARE OFFERED

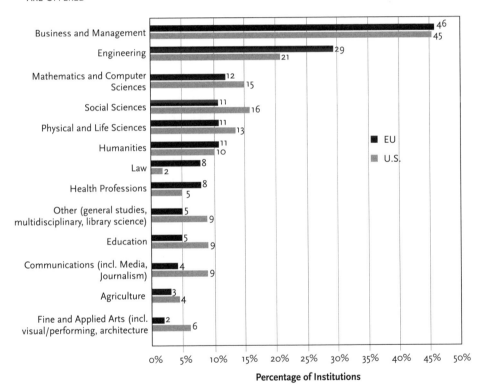

Source: Transatlantic Degree Programs Survey 2008

## Student Mobility

Both U.S. and European institutions report that more European students participate in their programs than U.S. students. However, that gap is much wider among EU institutions (1.2 U.S. students to 24.2 EU students) than it is for U.S. institutions (4.3 U.S. students to 9.6 EU students), indicating that many of the joint and double degree programs offered by responding EU institutions are done jointly with other EU partner institutions and cater largely to European students.

TABLE 3: NUMBER OF STUDENTS WHO PARTICIPATE ANNUALLY IN JOINT OR DOUBLE DEGREE PROGRAMS

|  | U.S. Institutions | | EU Institutions | |
|---|---|---|---|---|
|  | U.S. Students | EU Students | U.S. Students | EU Students |
| Mean | 4.3 | 9.6 | 1.2 | 24.2 |
| Median | 2 | 3 | 0 | 10 |
| Total # of Students | 238 | 530 | 101 | 2032 |

Source: Transatlantic Degree Programs Survey 2008

A majority of both U.S. and EU respondents report that students begin their studies at the home institution and then transfer to one (or more) participating institution(s) (Table 4). While this is the preference for both U.S. and EU institutions, the model is unquestionably the prevalent one in the EU, whereas in the U.S. it exists alongside other models to a greater extent.

Cohort models were the second most common, accounting for 26 percent of U.S. and 15 percent of EU responses. Other models were far less common, with very few respondents reporting that their programs enroll individual students who begin their studies at the foreign institution and then transfer to the home institution.

TABLE 4: PATTERNS OF STUDENT MOBILITY

|  | U.S. Respondents (%) | EU Respondents (%) |
|---|---|---|
| Students study at home institution first, then transfer to one (or more) participating institution(s). | 49 | 77 |
| All study as a cohort (they start in one location and then transfer together to other institutions). | 26 | 15 |
| All move back and forth as a national/institutional cohort (they start at different participating locations and do not form a global "program cohort"). | 14 | 5 |
| Students study at participating (foreign) institution first, then transfer to the home institution. | 11 | 4 |

Source: Transatlantic Degree Programs Survey 2008

Respondents were asked the minimum, maximum and average length of time spent at the institution abroad on their joint and double degree programs. The average response for minimum length abroad was 38 percent for U.S. respondents and 35 percent for EU respondents. The average maximum percentage of time spent abroad was 53 percent for U.S. respondents and 52 percent for EU respondents. These responses are very similar and indicate that, in general, programs on both sides of the Atlantic tend to send students abroad for between one-third and one-half of the total length of the program.

TABLE 5: PERIOD OF STUDY SPENT AT THE INSTITUTION(S) ABROAD

|  | U.S. Respondents | EU Respondents |
| --- | --- | --- |
| Minimum % | 38.3 | 34.9 |
| Maximum % | 52.5 | 52.0 |

Source: Transatlantic Degree Programs Survey 2008

## Funding and Tuition

A wide variation in funding structures for joint and double degree programs exists between U.S. and EU institutions. The greatest difference is the percentage of program costs accounted for by student fees between EU institutions (26 percent) and U.S. institutions (58 percent). To compensate for low student fees, EU institutions tend to draw more funding from university budgets (32 percent) and from external sources (40 percent), which include governments, foundations, and industry. U.S. institutions, on the other hand, reported far fewer contributions from university budgets (16 percent) and external sources (27 percent). At U.S. institutions, foreign governments accounted for about as much support as the U.S. government, whereas at EU institutions the home government tended to outspend foreign governments by a ratio of 2:1.

European institutions listed many more external funding sources than U.S. institutions. In addition to the Atlantis Program, which provides funding to both U.S. and EU institutions, European respondents indicated that the Erasmus and Erasmus Mundus Programs were a significant source of external funding. Other sources providing support to EU institutions included the German Academic Exchange Service (DAAD), national and regional governments, and the Deutsch-Französische Hochschule (Franco-German University). Very few U.S. institutions listed U.S. government funding sources other than the Atlantis Program.

Average Funding Sources for EU Institutions

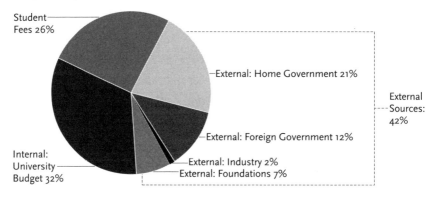

Average Funding Sources for U.S. Institutions

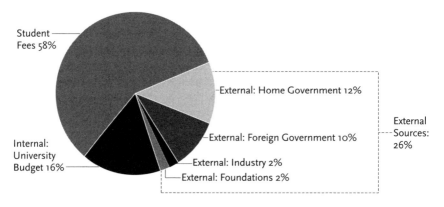

Source: Transatlantic Degree Programs Survey 2008

The majority of European respondents (64 percent) indicated that students paid all fees for the entire program to the home institution, with slightly fewer U.S. respondents indicating the same (55 percent). U.S. respondents were more likely to have programs in which the student paid separate tuition fees at each participating institution (31 percent) than EU respondents (16 percent).

Many respondents on both the U.S. and EU sides indicated that in many cases, both schemes apply, or that fees and fee structures vary for each program, often depending on the memorandum of understanding between partner institutions. Several respondents indicated that fees are paid to the "coordinating" institution, which then divides tuition revenues among partner institutions. Others have noted different approaches depending on the academic level. At the graduate level, students pay at each institution, whereas at the undergraduate level, students only pay at the home institution.

FIGURE 5: TUITION AND FEE STRUCTURE

EU Respondents

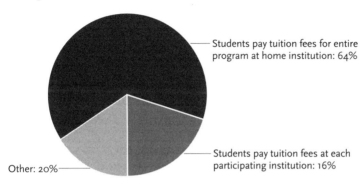

Students pay tuition fees for entire program at home institution: 64%

Students pay tuition fees at each participating institution: 16%

Other: 20%

U.S. Respondents

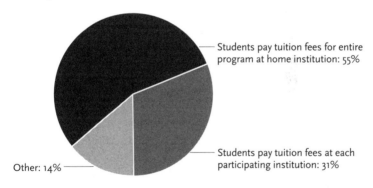

Students pay tuition fees for entire program at home institution: 55%

Students pay tuition fees at each participating institution: 31%

Other: 14%

Source: Transatlantic Degree Programs Survey 2008

## Program Language

According to survey respondents, English is by far the most commonly used language of instruction in joint or double degree programs. French, Spanish, German, and Italian round out the top five most widely used languages. French and German are the only languages other than English that are widely used as the principal language of instruction. Spanish and Italian, if used as languages of instruction, are almost always secondary languages in these programs (Figure 6).

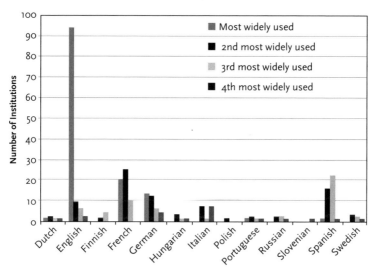

Source: Transatlantic Degree Programs Survey 2008

Nearly half of all programs (46 percent) included mandatory foreign language training at both the home and the partner institution. Fifteen percent offered training only at the home institution and 5 percent offered training only at the partner institution. Eight percent of responding institutions said that that the language of instruction was the same at the home and partner institution and therefore did not require foreign language training. About a quarter (26 percent) did not offer any language training at all.

The majority of responding institutions have ways of formally assessing foreign language acquisition; however, European institutions were more likely to formally assess language acquisition (73 percent) than U.S. institutions (58 percent). The higher percentage among EU institutions may partly be a result of a requirement by the EU Commission that mandates that Atlantis Program grantees assess language acquisition. On the U.S. side, formal language assessment is not currently required for Atlantis Program institutions but will be in future years.

## Selection Process and Recruitment

The basic method of student selection does not appear to vary between EU and U.S. institutions. Slightly less than half of all institutions select students separately but with shared criteria (48 percent EU; 45 percent U.S.), about one-third indicate that their programs use joint selection processes with all participating institutions (31 percent EU; 33 percent U.S.), and about one-fifth of respondents selected students separately from their partner institutions using different criteria (20 percent EU; 19 percent U.S.).

The most common way to recruit students to joint or double degree programs appears to be through the university/faculty website (72 percent), individual counseling and advising (62 percent), and brochures and flyers (59 percent). Several respondents indicated other effective outreach mechanisms, including information sessions and classroom visits, professional listservs and journals, and word of mouth.

Survey respondents were asked to elaborate on some of the key challenges in recruiting students. Most of the responding U.S. institutions commented on three central issues: language requirements (lack of foreign language proficiency), cost (program fees, limited availability of financial aid, instability in the dollar/euro exchange rate), and U.S. students' attitudes toward study abroad (according to comments from survey respondents, U.S. students are less likely to study abroad for a full semester or academic year, students do not see tangible value in studying abroad, and study abroad is not an integrated element in most academic disciplines, especially in the sciences).

Less frequently mentioned challenges in recruiting students were structural issues. However, several respondents noted challenges related to mismatched academic calendars, the need to ensure that students meet the stringent academic requirements, and articulating degree requirements and curricula.

Responses from European survey participants were quite similar and also revolved around high costs and the lack of required language skills (mostly among the American students they seek to attract). European respondents also frequently mentioned that a particular challenge was to find high-quality, motivated students who can meet the stringent prerequisites and high academic standards required for success in the program. Very few respondents specifically commented on issues related to the Bologna process. Only two respondents said that the number of students participating in study abroad has been declining.

## Program Evaluation and Accreditation

Nearly all respondents indicated that they offer some form of program or faculty evaluation. EU respondents were about as likely to be regularly evaluated by internal experts (52 percent) as external experts (50 percent), whereas U.S. respondents were more likely to be evaluated by internal experts (51 percent) than external experts (26 percent). Students were more likely to evaluate faculty members among EU respondents (62 percent) than among U.S. respondents (44 percent).

U.S. regional accrediting agencies were the most common method of accreditation for U.S. respondents (54 percent), followed by U.S. national accrediting agencies (36 percent). EU respondents were much more likely to be accredited by a Ministry of Education (51 percent) or an accrediting agency in an EU member state (45 percent). Somewhat more EU programs were not accredited (10 percent) compared to U.S. programs (2 percent).

TABLE 6: DEGREE PROGRAM ACCREDITATION

| | U.S. Respondents (%) | EU Respondents (%) |
|---|---|---|
| Accredited by U.S. regional accrediting agency | 54 | 7 |
| Accredited by U.S. national accrediting agency | 36 | 13 |
| Accredited by an agency in an EU member state | 16 | 45 |
| Professional accreditation/discipline-specific | 23 | 20 |
| Accredited by a Ministry of Education | 17 | 51 |
| Not accredited | 2 | 10 |

Source: Transatlantic Degree Programs Survey 2008. Individual respondents were permitted to select multiple accreditation methods.

## Program Initiation and Motivations

About half of all respondents indicated that initiating a joint degree program requires all levels of the institution to be involved, an opinion shared by slightly more U.S. respondents (57 percent) than EU respondents (48 percent). The second most common scenario for all respondents was the bottom-up approach, with 29 percent of U.S. respondents and 33 percent of EU respondents indicating that programs were mainly initiated through individual professors' activities with some institutional support. Few respondents said that programs were initiated through a top-down approach—14 percent of U.S. respondents and 19 percent of EU respondents.

Motivations for launching a joint or double degree program can be placed in the following rough order, from most important to least important:

1. Advancing internationalization of the campus

2. Raising international visibility and prestige of the institution

3. Broadening the institution's educational offerings

4. Strengthening academic research collaborations

5. Increasing foreign student enrollments

These motivating factors are generally the same for EU and U.S. institutions; however, it is interesting to note two cases where motivations vary slightly. As might be expected, EU institutions were more concerned about the Bologna process, with 80 percent of institutions saying it was either an "important" or "very important" factor, compared with 53 percent of U.S. institutions. Another interesting case was "increasing revenue," which 68 percent of EU respondents judged to be "not important" versus only 53 percent of U.S. respondents.

TABLE 7: RELATIVE IMPORTANCE OF MOTIVATING FACTORS TO LAUNCH A JOINT OR DOUBLE DEGREE PROGRAM

| | EU Institutions | | | U.S. Institutions | | |
|---|---|---|---|---|---|---|
| | Not Important | Important | Very Important | Not Important | Important | Very Important |
| Advancing internationalization of the campus | 6 | 29 | **65** | 0 | 25 | **75** |
| Raising international visibility and prestige of institution | 5 | 29 | **66** | 2 | 34 | **64** |
| Broadening our educational offerings | 1 | 45 | **54** | 15 | 40 | **46** |
| Strengthening academic research collaborations | 7 | 46 | **47** | 15 | 39 | **46** |
| Increasing foreign student enrollments | 9 | 44 | **47** | 15 | 42 | **43** |
| Responding to international mobility situation prompted by the Bologna process | 19 | **49** | 31 | **47** | 36 | 17 |
| Increasing revenue | **68** | 25 | 6 | **53** | 29 | 18 |

Source: Transatlantic Degree Programs Survey 2008

## Challenges

EU and U.S. respondents met with similar challenges in attempting to establish successful joint and double degree programs. Topping the list for both EU and U.S. institutions were securing adequate funding and ensuring sustainability of the program. Precise order of challenges varies after this but remains similar in most cases. Notable divergences include:

- Securing institutional support and deciding on the fee structure appear to be more challenging for U.S. than for EU institutions.

- EU institutions consider curriculum design to be more challenging than do U.S. institutions.

- Notably, both U.S. and EU institutions consider negotiating a memorandum of understanding to be one of their least difficult tasks when designing a joint or double degree program.

TABLE 8: POTENTIAL CHALLENGES IN SETTING UP JOINT OR DOUBLE DEGREE PROGRAMS
(1 BEING NOT CHALLENGING AT ALL, AND 5 BEING VERY CHALLENGING)

|  | EU | U.S. |
|---|---|---|
| Securing adequate funding | 3.5 | 3.9 |
| Ensuring sustainability of the program | 3.5 | 3.7 |
| Different requirements for general education | 3.3 | 3.2 |
| Designing the curriculum | 3.3 | 3 |
| Agreeing on credit transfer recognition | 3.2 | 3 |
| Resolving differences in academic calendars | 3.1 | 2.9 |
| Communicating with partner institution(s) | 3 | 3.1 |
| Recruiting students | 3 | 3.3 |
| Determining durations of degrees in each country | 2.8 | 2.8 |
| Getting the program accredited | 2.8 | 2.6 |
| Securing institutional support | 2.7 | 3.3 |
| Resolving language issues | 2.6 | 2.9 |
| Negotiating a Memorandum of Understanding | 2.6 | 2.2 |
| Deciding on the fee structure | 2.4 | 3 |

Source: Transatlantic Degree Programs Survey 2008

Survey respondents were asked to elaborate on the key challenges in establishing joint or double degree programs. Their answers are summarized below:

*Recruiting students:* Many respondents pointed to the difficulties they face in recruiting students to joint or double degree programs. The majority indicated that it is particularly problematic to find U.S. students interested in such programs. According to the survey respondents, this student flow imbalance, which is also well-known among more traditional student exchange programs, is likely caused by the fact that U.S. students are generally less inclined to study abroad than European students and often do not meet the required levels of language proficiency. As one of the survey respondents commented: "The key challenge is to recruit students with good linguistic competencies and the will to go abroad."

*Securing institutional support:* Challenges with securing institutional support figured very prominently among the responses. As some survey respondents pointed out, personal commitment by individual faculty is often the starting point of a joint or double degree program, but without institutional support on all levels, most such endeavors will be short lived. "Sustainability," as one respondent commented, "must be based on long-term institutional commitment." Or, as another respondent recalls: "Overall things went pretty smoothly, once the institutional support was given."

*Resolving differences:* In the context of institutional support, a number of participants also said they encountered major problems with their home institution's administration. In the words of one U.S. respondent: "Generally EU and U.S. partners are very eager to cooperate and collaborate but they sometimes insist about taking into account only their rules." Lack of understanding of a partner institution's realities and needs constitutes a serious challenge, according to several respondents. Reaching a win-win situation for two (or more) institutions might be impossible if the partners are not prepared to be flexible on some issues and if there is no real institutional vision to encourage such flexibility on all levels.

*Accreditation and quality assurance:* Numerous comments suggested major challenges with quality assurance and accreditation. While a relationship of mutual trust remains the single most important ingredient for successful joint or double degree programs according to the respondents, "a clear legal framework upon which to build these programs—including accreditation system guidelines—is also needed." One of the respondents puts it almost as a plea: "We are interested in having a large number of joint and dual degrees, but we are constantly turning down opportunities because the quality assurance burden is so great." In cases where formal accreditation of joint or double degrees is possible, it usually comes with increased costs both in terms of time and funding.

Some survey respondents criticized accreditation authorities on both sides of the Atlantic for their slow response and sometimes even unwillingness to acknowledge the realities of novel forms of international higher education cooperation such as joint or double degree programs. In addition, challenges can derive from differences in accreditation cultures. One respondent points out: "Accreditation systems vary because quality is defined with rigor but based on different approaches and perspectives."

*Funding:* Many respondents discussed challenges related to funding, both in terms of support for student mobility and overall program costs. Some responses suggest that without additional funding for a coordinator or program assistant it was difficult to meet the additional workload that joint or double degree programs usually generate. Funding for students, in the form of scholarships or travel grants, was another issue frequently mentioned by survey participants from both Europe and the U.S. In particular, many noted that few funding opportunities existed for U.S. students going abroad. For European students, respondents largely agreed, the main challenge in terms of costs was the issue of tuition fees at U.S. partner institutions, unless agreements for tuition waivers were in place.

Asked to provide suggestions about how challenges could be overcome, most respondents agreed that building up and maintaining good lines of communication both with the partner and with the home institution is crucial. As one respondent puts it: "Good advance planning and good ongoing communication between the partners are both key," as is "closely working with academic departments and university administration." A number of respondents also mentioned that flexibility from both sides is essential to overcoming challenges, adding that it all starts with a relationship of trust. According to one European respondent, it was largely "learning by doing—it goes easier and easier every time. Find out your institutions' and your academics' priorities—as well as your partners' priorities and then find the best possible solution. Everyone has to give up on something."

With regard to student recruitment challenges, respondents suggest that they need a clear understanding of who the potential students are and where they can be found. Since many joint and double degree programs are designed for the best and brightest only, institutions must develop a comprehensive strategy to target and successfully recruit these students.

## Future Plans

A large majority of both U.S. institutions (87 percent) and EU institutions (85 percent) plan to continue to develop more joint and double degrees. The institutions that indicated they are not planning to develop more degree programs generally said that the institution currently had different priorities and that international alliances would be expanded based on particular strategic goals. Several also noted the lack of resources, administrative burdens involved in setting up collaborative degree programs, and the lack of institutional support.

Surveyed institutions are very interested in developing further programs in countries in Europe, North America, Latin America, and East Asia. There appears to be less interest in developing programs with institutions in the Middle East or Africa. The most desired partner countries for EU institutions were the United States, China, Germany, Canada, and the United Kingdom. Preferred partner countries for U.S institutions were China, India, Germany, and France.

## Conclusion

The survey results presented in this article do not claim to be representative of all existing joint or double degree programs in the transatlantic context, let alone similar programs between partner institutions in other world regions. Each and every collaborative degree program is unique. Naturally, all programs exist in specific academic and administrative settings, with a variety of institutional provisions and legal realities that may enhance or discourage their development. Hence, the challenges they face will be equally diverse, making it difficult to offer advice on best practices and guidelines.

However, as the survey results clearly indicate, certain tendencies and overarching commonalities can be identified. With regard to the transatlantic context, despite numerous challenges articulated by survey participants, it is very unlikely that the next few years will see less development of collaborative degree programs between European and U.S. institutions. Other countries and regions are also seeing growth: China, for instance, ranked number one when U.S. respondents were asked with which countries they wanted to develop more collaborative programs in the future, and it ranked number two among EU respondents. Similar developments, albeit on a different scale, can also be observed for other world regions, in particular other parts of Asia and South America. Nonetheless, at present the transatlantic link prevails as the dominant connection in the realm of collaborative joint or double degree programs, in large part thanks to key funding initiatives such as the EU-U.S. Atlantis Program that supports the development of such programs.

This survey did not attempt to focus on student preferences or to address their specific concerns. Its goal was rather to assess the current landscape of collaborative degree programs in the transatlantic context, an assessment that should be expanded in the future. As we attempt to understand further aspects of these programs, the student perspective should receive more attention. For example, future research could include a survey of alumni of joint and double degree programs addressing their employment opportunities upon the completion of their degree. Addressing the students' perspective in turn might prove crucial for developing successful recruitment strategies.

# Rationales and Strategies behind Double Degrees: A Transatlantic Approach

By Pascal Delisle

As noted in the previous chapter, "Joint and Dual Degree Programs in the Transatlantic Context: A Survey Report," transatlantic joint and especially double degrees are on the rise. Behind this general trend, what are the underlying purposes for universities to enter into such close collaboration? These purposes are not always clearly stated, nor even entirely conscious on part of the stakeholders. Based on years of experience setting up such double degrees and advising universities on both sides of the Atlantic, I try to address this question first by explaining the broader asymmetrical context in which this trend emerges and second by submitting a very rough typology of double degrees, based on their purpose and on their main features. Finally, I suggest where the current frontier stands on this matter, with the emergence of what one could call "global" double degrees. An important footnote has to do with the difficulty in characterizing Europe as a whole in its relation to the United States. In particular, the situation of Great Britain is closer to that of the United States than it is to the situation of its fellow European partners.

## Asymmetrical Transatlantic Context

Higher education and research systems are increasingly engaging in both competition and cooperation across the globe. This takes place to a certain extent at the systemic level, for example, with the Lisbon agenda for the European Union and the America Competes Act in the United States. Competition and cooperation mostly take place at the level of individual institutions. Double degrees are clearly an expression of this two-sided logic of competition and cooperation. In addressing the question of double degrees between European and American institutions, the specifics of the transatlantic context need to be taken into account.

- The context in which double degrees emerge is not a neutral one composed of two similar geographical ensembles between which universities are to develop partnerships. One needs to keep in mind that for most stakeholders in research and higher education, the American higher education system continues to be seen as the anchor. This perception is surely often distorted or exaggerated as the reality of American higher education is one of great diversity, including in levels of internationalization. This dominant perception, however, reflects the fundamental strength and breadth of the American research and higher education system. This certainly gives American institutions a competitive edge in developing international partnerships to their liking. This difference in perceived status, in my opinion, does partly shape the purposes for which double degrees are established.

- For prestigious American institutions, the idea of building double degrees with European institutions was long seen as irrelevant. Currently, the development of such double degrees, even by some of the most prestigious American institutions, indicates a growing shift in institutional approaches to international cooperation. Partnerships are increasingly seen as a win-win situation, even when the prestige and attractiveness of the American institution is superior to that of its European counterpart. At stake is the preparation of graduates for an increasingly international and intercultural job market as well as the recent awareness that higher education has become a more competitive environment in which resting on a position of superiority is no longer a viable strategy.

- The broader American context of reflection and concern about the fragile status of American science and technology and the emergence of new global competitors also pushes in that direction. I do not dwell here on the roots of this shift as they are well documented in many reports and analyses published in the last decade by the National Academies, the National Science Board, and the Rand Corporation, among others.

- As a result, in the last 10 years we have seen a shift in the U.S., including at some of the most prestigious American universities, toward closer partnerships with European counterparts. Many less-prestigious American universities do feel the same growing urge to develop these collaborations, of which double degrees are an important part. For those institutions, this is also a way to differentiate themselves on the higher education market, by offering innovative programs that add value to the education of their students and therefore reinforce their own attractiveness compared to more prestigious universities. The same combination of rationales applies to European universities, with one important additional element: with the U.S. higher education system as the reference, the motivation of European universities to get into such partnerships with American universities is even stronger.

## A Rough Typology of Double Degrees

Typologies are always a perilous endeavor, as reality contains elements of both continuity and radical difference. I submit here a very simple typology between research-driven double degrees, where students and professors alike are part of a broad partnership, and professional education-based double degrees, in which students and administrators are the key stakeholders.

## Research-Driven Double Degrees

- Research-driven double degrees (at the master's level in most cases, the PhD level in some) appear to be fairly symmetrical in their purpose. Given the big difference in the structure of PhD programs between countries, the involvement and ownership of faculty in setting up dual PhD degrees is all the more necessary, as administrators cannot impose such initiatives on their faculty. Complementarities of approaches and methods allow partners to better equip their graduates for a largely globalized job market. In addition, this type of partnership widens the reciprocal institutional learning process by which each university acquires, over time, a broader research capacity, and faculty reach new horizons in their research.

- Engineering, to my knowledge, is a field in which professors are strongly involved in transatlantic collaboration and where joint education initiatives emerge from research collaborations. Although knowledge about the history and details of double degrees is scarce, the fact that, according the IIE/FUB report, engineering is the second field in which transatlantic double degrees have emerged indicates to us that research-driven double degrees are widespread.

- In these cases, academic rationales tend to dominate. As part of this win-win game, both participating students and the academic departments or schools involved learn through the process: new methods, expansion of the disciplinary scope of the department, but also availability of specific types of equipment, ability to explore synergies with other departments or centers, etc. Strategic concerns at the level of the university as a whole are not necessarily a main factor in setting up such double degrees, as specialized faculty are in the driver's seat and may not be as sensitive to the logistics of international competition and cooperation beyond their own field.

- Of course, all double degrees require approval at a central level of the institution (faculty senate, deans, provost or even the state legislature, depending on the university), and one should not underestimate the difficulty of reaching such agreements—especially, in the American context, at public universities, where an additional layer of approval is required before any such agreement is signed. At the institutional level too, contextual considerations of prestige, "branding," ranking, and perception do have an impact. But the soundness of the proposal, the reality of research and academic complementarities figure very strongly.

- Moreover, in the social sciences, faculty worldviews more deeply influenced by the paradigm of international relations seem to translate to a higher degree of prudence in building joint and double degrees. Social science faculty are more highly concerned about the perceived level of a partner university, as if sovereignty over degrees could only be shared between equals.

**CASE STUDY:**

**Lille University of Science and Technology (USTL), France, and Georgia Institute of Technology Dual Master of Science Degree in Nanotechnology, Electrical and Computer Engineering**

The strong research partnership established over the years between these two universities (as well as with the Georgia Tech Campus in eastern France) led in 2007 to the establishment of a dual degree. With the support of the Partner University Fund (PUF) at the French Embassy in Washington, D.C., this program allows participating master's students to earn a Master of Science in Electrical and Computer Engineering from Georgia Tech and the "Diplôme National de Master Nano et Micro Technologie" from USTL. This program has two parts: a three-semester academic program taking place at Georgia Tech Atlanta, Georgia Tech Metz (the Georgia Tech Campus in France), and USTL, as well as a six- to nine-month internship in the U.S. and Europe. This partnership is based on preexisting courses and benefits from the existing infrastructure of distance learning. About 20 percent of the courses are delivered by distance learning, thanks to the extensive distance learning network existing at Georgia Tech.

## Professional Education-Based Double Degrees

- Professional schools (international and public affairs, business, law, journalism, etc.) are certainly involved in research, and their teachings are rooted in research to different degrees. However, when it comes to setting up double degrees, their motivations are, in my experience, largely nonacademic. They have first to do with their capacity to best prepare their students for the increasingly global job market. Mastering other languages and understanding how to do business or conduct public affairs on another continent are crucial to this purpose. Since business and management are, according to the IIE report, the main fields of study for double degrees, I sense that professional education-based double degrees represent the majority of transatlantic double degrees.

- Few students, however, are taking part in such double degrees at any given moment, so if this were the sole purpose of the double degree, one would wonder why universities make such an effort to set them up. The answer to this question is two-sided. On the one hand, most nonparticipating students benefit from the existence of double degrees, since through them their university degree acquires a higher level of recognition and "international convertibility." For instance, seeing your master's degree compared to one from a prestigious foreign university anchors the reputation of your own university degree. These "branding" or "anchoring" benefits weigh substantially, in my experience, in the decision of university executives to enter into such double degrees, even more so when this double degree is established with an institution perceived to be more prestigious than their own. Additionally, as several major international rankings place positive value on program internationalization, these degrees bring a double dividend to the universities, as the proportion of international students increases as well.

- Setting up such double degrees does not need to heavily involve faculty research and teaching activities, even though their involvement may bring additional benefits, as the students are the ones integrating the complementarities of the two systems in their training experience. As participating students learn from their dual experience, the institutions do not necessarily expand their scope of expertise, methods, and research beyond their capacity to administer such programs. In other words, we are still in a win-win game, but the students are the main beneficiaries, whereas the departments or schools involved do not necessarily "grow" internally from the experience. In some regulated professions, law in particular, one additional motivation is added to the equation: double degrees provide easier access to such regulated professions in the partner's country.

- Professional education-based double degrees are rarely built on joint research. Over time, such collaborations can nurture stronger academic relations between the partners, but this is not a precondition for setting up these double degrees. These programs are usually limited to the bachelor's and master's levels and are often driven by dynamic administrators, vice presidents, or presidents. These administrators are not specialists in the concerned field but are acutely aware of the changing global context of national and international job markets for young professionals. They often show vision and leadership in the way they use such tools to maximize the prestige and reputation of their own institution and can leverage internationalization as a tool to profoundly transform and reform their own institutions.

- University executives and administrators need to remain fully involved downstream, as difficult questions of credit transfer, visas, degree requirements, and internships may arise. Schools with strong administrative governance can excel in this even when their faculties are lightly involved. In some cases, however, especially in the case of "non-horizontal" double degrees (MA/JD, BA/MA for instance), administrators need strong support and backing from the faculty. Although administrators usually remain the proactive players in the process, faculty support is necessary for the resolution of very difficult curricular problems.

- For dynamic (though less prestigious) institutions, double degrees can be a way to boost attractiveness to students and compete even with more prestigious institutions in their own country. These double degrees, in other words, appear as crucial tools for differentiating one's academic programs from those of other schools. As in the case of monopolistic competition in market economics, this increasing differentiation of degree offerings through double degrees can lead to a different, less hierarchical kind of competition, where different schools can excel in different areas.

- Double degrees will most likely continue to thrive:
    - As long as graduates from these programs see their job opportunities improve;
    - As long as non-double degree students reap the benefits from the positive externalities provided from those double degrees (i.e., better "international convertibility" of their degree and better recognition of their university in particular); and
    - As long as the institutions are satisfied by the increased prestige and better rankings that result in most cases.
- The asymmetry in the transatlantic context, noted above, does play out strongly in those cases, as administrators try to partner with similarly prestigious institutions. In a context of real or perceived superiority of the American higher education system, European universities find a specific interest in those double degrees as a key in a global strategy to position themselves as world class universities. The fruits of this acquired status, obtained through this "American detour," can then be harvested globally, in Europe, Asia, or elsewhere. In a sense, whereas many European universities started quite logically with a European strategy, responding to the incentives offered by the European Union, for some universities, an American strategy could be rightly seen as the first step of a global strategy.

## CASE STUDY:

### Columbia University and the London School of Economics Dual Master in Public Affairs (MPA)

Since the early 2000s, Columbia University's School of International and Public Affairs (SIPA) and the London School of Economics and Political Science (LSE) have offered their respective students the possibility to earn MPA degrees from both SIPA and the LSE in the same amount of time it takes to earn one degree. Students are recruited during their first year of studies at each of the two MPA programs, go through a selection process and then proceed to spend their second year at the partner university. Curricula on both sides are unchanged, and students draw the benefits from this program both in terms of exposure to different educational experiences and pedagogical traditions, as well as access to enhanced career opportunities in Europe and the United States. This is a good example of a professional education-based dual degree and is probably one of the least shaped by the asymmetrical transatlantic context mentioned above because the European partner university is British.

## A Third Way: "Global" Double Degrees

Up to now, most double degree programs have evolved from existing degree programs in each of the partner institutions. Once established, the double degree program would recruit students from within each of the two programs. Students from one university would apply (and sometimes fiercely compete) to enter into the double degree program and obtain a second degree at the end of the process. One could refer to those double degrees, for lack of a better word, as "international" double degrees. There is, however, a third model slowly emerging that I call the "global" double degree.

- Today, a small but increasing proportion of students are thinking globally about their training and careers. For them, finding the right match, upstream, between the content of a program and its international "nature" is becoming a priority. Many of these students have already experienced, in one way or another, some form of cross-border education, either because they come from international families or because they have acquired this awareness through a prior experience of study abroad or exchange. They see their own identity as multilayered and feel at ease in multinational groups of students looking at international career opportunities in the broad context of cultural and economic globalization.

- For these students, a third family of double degrees is proving increasingly attractive: the "global" double degree. This new type of double degree derives from an assessment made by some key faculty and administrators at leading institutions: there is room to jointly design double degrees that are finely tuned to the demands of the market and attract the kind of students described above through innovative recruitment procedures. Instead of recruiting students from specific degree programs within each university, recruitment can take place jointly and worldwide and be managed by a joint task force between the two institutions. Once recruited, students follow a curriculum designed jointly by the two universities taking place on both campuses and are awarded both degrees at the end of the process. Such programs are clearly on the side of professional education-based double degrees.

- One additional benefit from this model has to do with the way in which tuition disparities between countries can be managed in "global" double degrees. Whereas in "international" double degrees, students join their university with clear expectations in terms of tuition fees, entering into a double degree program often has an impact on the total cost of their studies, depending on how the double degree is structured. Moreover, students in these traditional double degrees tend to fall between the cracks when it comes to obtaining financial aid or work-study support through their university, as the programs are not designed for them. However, when recruiting for a "global" double degree, representatives of both universities are able to present the candidates with a clear and already established tuition structure. They are also able to build financial aid upstream in the double degree, allowing the students to have better access to the different forms of support.

- Such a level of collaboration between institutions is rare and can only derive from years of common work leading to full recognition of the collaborating universities as strategic partners with whom "sovereignty" over academic affairs and degrees can be shared. To my knowledge, there are only a few of them at this stage. One important advantage of this model of jointly designed double degrees is that they do not need to be tied to existing degree programs—not only because students are not recruited from them but also because their purpose is largely to meet a new demand not yet met by existing programs.

- However, how to handle such groups of students while catering to the "regular" students is not always an easy task for the host university. Not only do universities want to transmit part of the traditional identity to this group of students and avoid the "island" scenario, but it is also a matter of not giving the other students the feeling that they are a second-rate group. This is certainly something administrators and faculty alike need to learn how to manage. The same applies concerning the alumni status of those graduates, as they will have spent "only" part of the time other students spend on campus.

## CASE STUDY:

### Sciences Po/Georgetown Law Dual Degree in International Affairs (MIA) and Law

In 2008, Georgetown University Law School and Sciences Po (France) have launched a Dual Master of International Affairs and Law (MIA/LLM) open to candidates from around the world. Recognizing the importance of preparing lawyers and policymakers to function in a global environment, Georgetown and Sciences Po are offering this dual degree for students who have completed a law degree that satisfies the academic requirements for practicing as a lawyer in the country where they studied. Recruiting students from all over the world, this dual master's degree takes advantage of the comparative advantage of each university in its area of excellence, creating a program that each institution would have been unable to set up on its own. Students spend their first year at Sciences Po in Paris doing coursework in international affairs and their second year in Washington completing the Master of Law (LLM) curriculum. Having a cohort of students going from one university to the other also makes it possible to make specific adjustments on requirements, decided jointly and upstream between the universities. Application is made through the Sciences Po online international admission process and a joint admission board.

If European universities have shown a particular dynamism in this drive toward traditional or "international" double and joint degrees, studies confirm that American universities are now also fully aware of the benefits of such arrangements (see the 2007 and 2008 Council of Graduate Schools (CGS) International Graduate Admission Survey II: Final Applications and Initial Offers of Admission). As many institutions follow the trend, more benefits will be harvested by universities and students alike. As joint and double degrees continue to multiply, a wider pool of students will benefit from them instead of a small number of privileged ones. From the perspective of universities, this also means that the competitive advantage enjoyed by the first movers will progressively decline, leading the most dynamic of them toward a new frontier of competition in cross-border education, of which global double degrees are certain to be a part.

| | Research-driven double degrees | Professional education-based double degrees | Global double degrees |
|---|---|---|---|
| Driver | Faculty-led<br>Academic rationales prevail | Administration-led<br>Prestige and/or job market rationales prevail | Administration-led<br>Prestige and/or job market rationales prevail |
| Advantages | Double degree students: quality of training, career opportunities<br><br>University and professors: Enhanced research capability<br><br>Faculty from both sides: Easy to agree on academic priorities<br><br>Professors and administrators: Easy to organize the recruitment process from their own program<br><br>Easy to design new elements of curriculum if faculty is leading the process | Double degree students: quality of training, career opportunities<br><br>Non-double degree students: Enhanced prestige of home university, better career opportunities<br><br>Administrators: Easy to organize the recruitment process<br><br>Administrators: Building blocks of the double degree are preexisting, little need to involve faculty in designing the program<br><br>University: Prestige and attractiveness, proportional to the asymmetry of the transatlantic context and to the individual prestige of the partner university | Double degree students: Program specifically designed to meet market demand<br><br>Course requirements, financial aid, logistics: Tailor-made<br><br>Non-double degree students: Enhanced prestige of home university, better career opportunities<br><br>Administrators: Broad pool of applicants<br><br>University: Prestige and attractiveness, proportional to the asymmetry of the transatlantic context and to the individual prestige of the partner university |
| Disadvantages | Course requirements, financial aid, and logistics need to be addressed afterwards, or retrofitted with the support of the administration<br><br>Administrators need to be aware of the specific needs of students<br><br>Some courses or modules need to be developed<br><br>Small pool of applicants | Course requirements, financial aid, and logistics need to be addressed afterwards, or retrofitted without creating opposition from the faculty<br><br>Faculty need to be aware of the specific needs of students<br><br>Little mutual learning occurs between the faculty of the two institutions<br><br>Small pool of applicants | When trying to address specific market expectations, need to design new elements of curriculum with faculty<br><br>Need to design ad hoc recruitment tools<br><br>Need to handle a broad range of students with different expectations: Housing, , pedagogy, career services, etc.<br><br>Need to avoid an "island" scenario in relation to other students |

# JOINT AND DOUBLE DEGREE PROGRAMS: CHANGING MOTIVATIONS

BY STEPHAN GEIFES

Joint and double degree programs play a major role in most recent discussions about internationalization strategies of higher education, especially in the transatlantic context. A conference of the EU Commission in Berlin in September 2006 even went as far to ask "Joint Degrees – A Hallmark of the European Education Area?"

The interest in these programs is not entirely new but they have enjoyed a different popularity over the last three decades. The aim of this short article is to point out the different—and changing—motivations stimulating the discourse about these programs and their realization within the general internationalization strategies in higher education.

In Europe, when the idea of joint and double degree programs came up in the 1980s, there were two major motivations. First of all, it aimed at solving the question of recognition of time spent and credits acquired abroad. A second strong driving force for joint and double degree programs was the need to solve problems of diploma recognition among European countries and ease access problems to labor markets.

These ideas were particularly strong in Europe in the context of the construction of the European Union in the 1980s. But at the same time, they were not easy to realize. That may be the reason why other solutions were preferred, and the development of joint and double degree programs stagnated.

On the one hand, through the creation of the Erasmus program at the end of the 1980s, "lighter" forms of cooperation were established. In particular, the ECTS credit system served to clear the way for credit recognition and transfer. Since its foundation, the Erasmus program has proved an unprecedented success: It enabled more than a million students to study abroad for a significant period of time. On the other hand, with ongoing European integration, access to labor markets gradually became less of a problem as it was guaranteed by a variety of EU legal regulations.

These developments were amplified by the Bologna process starting in 1999. Implementing similar bachelor and master degree structures in all European countries and ensuring diploma comparability was an integral part of the European Higher Education Area which the participating country wanted to create.

All these elements—Erasmus, ECTS, legal recognition, and the Bologna process—were not encouraging for the further development of joint and double degree programs. At the beginning of the new millennium, people saw the future of international exchange, at least in Europe, as a regular pattern of students doing their bachelor's degrees in one country and then moving on to another country to study for their master's degrees. While this may be possible and true for some, for the majority of students this is still theoretical.

The second half of the first decade of the 21$^{st}$ century has witnessed a revival—not only in Europe—of joint and double degree programs. Why? Not for the reasons these programs have initially been designed and created—solving problems of recognition and access to labor markets. The true reason for the success of these programs lies elsewhere. The completion of a joint or double degree enabled graduates to work abroad not only in legal terms, but even more importantly, spending a significant part of their study program abroad provided them with the skills needed to live and work in a different culture.

This has been demonstrated by joint and double degree programs encouraged by the French and German governments for 20 years now, from 1989 to 1999 through the Franco-German Higher Education College and since then by the Franco-German University. Today, about 5,000 students are enrolled in more than 150 programs supported by the Franco-German University. Every year, more than 1,000 obtain a joint or double degree in nearly all disciplines.

As globalization is gaining momentum, more and more students are studying abroad. With a reputation of being academically and personally extremely demanding, joint and double degree programs might not prove to be mass movers. What some call an impediment in recruiting critical numbers of students, others refer to as a guarantee for success in attracting the most talented ones. Due to their demanding admittance requirements, many joint or double degree programs have become elite programs. With increasing numbers of internationally mobile students, simply studying abroad might not do the trick any longer for ambitious students. They will increasingly look for offers that stick out of the sea of normal exchange programs and offer them a competitive advantage over their peers.

The growing number of such transatlantic programs, with exchange in both ways, can be regarded as a confirmation of this interpretation: U.S. and Canadian students might not necessarily be interested in access to European labor markets, but they will be attracted by elite programs.

Laying the Foundation – From Communication to Curriculum Design

# Securing Institutional Support for Doctoral Degree Collaborations: Addressing Policy, Procedural, and Financial Issues

By Nora Bonnin and Allan Lerner

Currently, research universities, especially public research universities, are under considerable pressure as they seek to maintain their research strengths and the vigor of their doctoral programs despite declining funds. More than ever, institutional regimens are being fortified to assure that resources are allocated wisely and managed carefully, and that they efficiently advance the institutional mission. Successfully proposing international doctoral degree collaborations in such an institutional climate requires that critical issues be thoroughly addressed on three levels: policy, procedural, and financial. In the limited space of this paper we seek to identify issues likely to emerge at each level of institutional consideration and likely to be critical in securing institutional support.

International doctoral collaborations can yield enormous benefits, provided that universities undertake such collaborations with strategic understanding and operational clarity. However, if the proposed collaboration is poorly thought through or the degree program poorly designed, if partners are not carefully chosen and partnerships properly gestated, if implementation is not scrupulous, or if the financial model is not thoroughly and transparently worked through, then considerable harm can affect the interests of all parties. Moreover, public research universities can expect especially vocal external challenges to expanding international agendas in times of state budgetary strains.

It is only to be expected that strong research institutions will apply rigorous evaluation processes to proposals for collaborative doctoral programs. In turn, strong proposals should expect full institutional support upon the successful completion of such processes.

"Why?" is a question that resonates louder at each successive level of review in a large, public research university. The answer for every proposal is normally considered most obvious at the level of the proposal's origination. It becomes progressively a more open question through subsequent levels of review, as broader institutional considerations are brought to bear. Advocates of doctoral degree collaboration with a foreign partner should be able to answer the "why" question on multiple levels, transposing answers to the perspectives characterizing each successive level of review.

Departments must be convinced that a research program will be strengthened, strong students will be recruited and graduated, and the department's contribution to its discipline will be strengthened. Colleges, integrating the work of disciplines, must see international collaborations as representing *significant* growth for a unit while preserving reasonably *balanced* growth across departments. Colleges must also see that administrative responsibilities and financial liabilities are realistically assessed in the age of revenue-centered management practices and that there are clear grounds for trust in the partner's capabilities and commitments as well. Overall, colleges must determine that what will be achieved through collaboration is worth the initial development effort and continuous undertaking and that it cannot be achieved more simply, directly, and safely as a program offered solely by the proposing institution.

While there is a general consensus on the value of internationalizing U.S. campuses, proposals for doctoral collaborations with foreign partners can raise complex issues that test the institution in ways that go far beyond what is required by simple increases in undergraduate study abroad figures. For doctoral degree collaborations, institutions must be thoroughly convinced of significant research merit, long-term financial soundness, administrative feasibility, strategic significance, reputational security, and manageable risk, comprehensively defined. Doctoral degree collaborations are therefore likely to be few in number and very high in institutional significance. External institutional reviewers must be convinced of the overall soundness of the institution's conclusions in these respects, as well as the suitability of the proposed doctoral collaboration given the profile of the institution and its strategic mission and priorities.

A major strategic choice that conditions the context of all proposal evaluation at the policy, procedural, financial, and strategic levels is whether the international doctoral collaboration will offer a multi-institutional degree (MID) or dual degrees (DDs). An MID program, sometimes referred to as a joint program, is one in which two or more universities pool their efforts to offer a curriculum collectively. An MID program leads to a single degree awarded by all institutions involved. Thus, the single diploma awarded to students of such programs lists the names of the two or more cooperating institutions and confers one degree. A DD program refers to an arrangement in which two universities individually award their own largely similar, if not identical, academic degrees to the student who completes overlapping curricula, each curriculum drawn from one of the collaborating institutions. It is the combined, overlapping program of study that constitutes the curriculum of the "dual degree program."

Typically, for dual degree programs, the sum of the student's coursework at both institutions is significantly less than what would be required if each institution's degree program were completed independently. However, while substantially truncated compared to the sum of two completely separate degree programs, dual degree programs nonetheless require more than the amount of academic work required for one degree alone. Thus, they remain inherently redundant in their academic requirements—compared to what each institution would normally require for the demonstration of academic competence in a given field at a given degree level.

*Redundancy* is often driven by a desire to justify awarding two degrees. *Truncation* is often driven by the desire to make the dual degree program attractive and feasible for students. Dual degree programs are inherently vulnerable to excess in either direction.

MIDs create the possibility of combining the resources of separate institutions to deliver a degree program that neither offers independently. Used sparingly and wisely, the MID can be a vital strategic tool for building university excellence internationally. This approach allows for relatively rapid development of doctoral programs in new academic fields; it is also consistent with a growing trend toward consortium-based research and the shared administration and use of research facilities in the sciences.

MIDs require the institution to accept the abstract and fundamental notion of sharing the authority to confer a degree with another institution. This notion must be accepted by the appropriate authorities of (and over) each of the participating institutions. DDs allow institutions to retain independence in conferring the degree, but they do so at the price of introducing redundancy and the related tension between excessive truncation and excessive duplication of overlapping curricula. DDs also pose the risk of credential inflation.

The policy decision to pursue doctoral degree collaboration via MIDs or DDs is fundamental to all stages of institutional consideration and therefore to the garnering of institutional support. MIDs certainly, and DDs very possibly, may also require the authorization of external bodies to which the institution must answer; e.g., boards, state commissions, and accreditors. However, regardless of the choice ultimately made between MID and DD approaches, international doctoral collaborations must be structured, defended, conducted, and evaluated according to a process that all institutions can support.

Each institution considering collaborative degrees will ultimately follow its own institutional protocol. However, an international agreement that involves a degree, and which may involve a new format for offering a degree or degrees collaboratively, may require the synthesis of protocols from several institutions. In this paper we focus on issues and concerns common to most American public research institutions, as well as which of these concerns should be reflected in whatever protocol is ultimately applied. We note key issues applicable at four cumulative levels: the academic unit, the college, the institution, and the institutional overseer(s).

Like most international collaborations, degree collaborations usually begin with the advocacy of a primary faculty champion. Such faculty often start out seeking "informal" support at multiple levels as they begin to hold the first discussions within the department. This stage is not too early to communicate clearly to such champions that collaborations must not only be feasible but desirable because they represent a potential for *credible, significant addition* to current institutional capabilities. Thus, enhancing an individual laboratory through the continued flow of a small number of outstanding graduate students may be a worthy ambition, but one perhaps better achieved through institutional means less complicated than a new MID or DD system. To be worth the struggle, faculty should be focused on creating significant innovation—whether in graduate professional education, research, or applied research with potential for significant industry applications such as important translational research. A related key issue is why the new program should be undertaken with a partner, or with the particular partner(s) proposed.

In the culture of public research universities, international degree collaborations are commonly judged according to standards not applied to existing degree programs offered by the home institution on its campus. As major institutional innovations, MIDs and DDs will receive sharper scrutiny, which is both their vulnerability and their strength as early proponents seek to gain broader support.

MIDs and DDs are also likely to be evaluated as initiatives lasting a fixed number of years, measured in program cohorts, rather than as permanent university programs. This is always the case when a partner institution is linked to the project through a contractual agreement, one which inevitably must allow for its own dissolution with notice. Collaborative degree programs are not mergers or acquisitions. They are, however, major commitments meriting extensive review. As a result, the review process is likely to place a premium on identifying significant institutional advantages to be had through such degree arrangements, beyond intellectual appropriateness. They will be permanent authorizations, yet likely to have a finite duration. The prospect of constructive innovation through cooperation then becomes a central component of the successful proposal. This and feasibility—in several senses—remain the overarching criteria for potential supporters. These questions should immediately be put to the departmental champions as an exercise in collegial "tough love." They will be asked at higher levels.

Thus, protocols for review should require that the issues of significant innovation, administrative and financial feasibility, and sustainability be posed during early discussions at the departmental level, though definitive solutions need not be elaborated yet. However, protocols should immediately identify the lead faculty for the development phase of the collaboration. Such review procedures should also describe the presumed goals of the program for the partner institution as well as the goals for the home institution, separately and jointly, as the case may be. This implies that the institutional profile and relevant strategic interests of the partner institution should be stated in detail in the home institution's review protocols.

It is also critical that the department, with as much hierarchical consultation as needed, be able to describe whether an MID or DD approach is best under the circumstances and to explain the relative advantages of both forms of collaboration in strengthening the department. This will normally entail a detailed explanation of how weaknesses at the home campus are offset by strengths at the proposed collaborating institution. We will simply note here that higher-level reviewers may question whether simply establishing new visibility in a particular foreign country is not better addressed through means simpler than collaborative degrees.

Departmental proposals seeking support at the college level must present strong evidence of the proposed project's financial feasibility and contribution to the strategic priorities of the college. Colleges are often the major financial accountability centers in large public research universities (Kirp, 2003). However, colleges are normally also the final major arbiters of the academic soundness of proposed new curricula or academic collaborations. Additional levels of review normally focus on administrative aspects of academic and financial decisions, rather than fresh consideration of academic soundness by the college. Beyond the college, the institutional attractiveness of the partner, the potential for significant academic innovation, the financial and legal soundness, administrative coherence and feasibility, and the institutional strategic value of the proposed collaboration will determine the support decision.

Thus, by the end of a college-level review, a supportive college should be able to serve as an informed participant in subsequent structured dialogues at the institutional level and beyond—both with subsequent institutional reviewers and the foreign partner. Such dialogue takes place on two fronts: academic (in conceptual terms) and administrative (in legal, financial, and administrative process terms). A key result of such dialogue should be a college description of quality assurance procedures for aspects of the proposed degree collaboration. The institutional partners will describe such procedures in the contracts governing their collaboration.

Reviewers beyond the college should normally require supporting data on the domestic and international academic market, applicable industry demand, and relationship to existing degrees offered by the partners and by comparable institutions. Also essential for collaborative degrees, proposals must describe key features in detail: prerequisites, credit values, language(s) of instruction, exhibits of the credentials to be conferred, transcript information, and any nationally required additional documentation depending on the partner institution. Further discussion of this important dimension of institutional articulation issues for MIDs and DDs, such as EU diploma supplements, wording of diplomas, etc.), is beyond the scope of this article (See Reinalda & Kulesza, 2005). Suffice it to say that contracts between the institutional partners must clearly describe all such relevant issues. They must be vetted in the review process at each home institution and will likely enter the bilateral institutional negotiations, which must be coordinated with the review process. No responsible institution can support a degree program in abstract without a thorough understanding of its operation and relevant details acknowledged by both institutions. These are ultimately issues of quality assurance.

Program sustainability is a related major concern for institutional reviewers of MID and DD proposals. All levels of review, but particularly the institutional and external overseer levels, understandably seek to support only major degree undertakings that can be expected to endure long enough to justify the effort to vet and establish them. Cohort-delimited programs that confer degrees through a contractual arrangement must nonetheless guarantee a minimum series of cohorts sufficient to justify conferring a permanent degree authority. A substantial sustainability case must be made for all MIDs and DDs.

Budgetary aspects of these concerns often require documentation to satisfy institutional authorities beyond the frequent contacts of college business managers. Determination of tuition levels, indirect or "spill-over" institutional costs, value of foreign in-kind contributions, and related budget quantities are ultimately institutional-level judgments. However, colleges should be expected to propose credible quantitative starting points for these items. Libraries, international units, student support systems, admissions and registrations systems, counseling systems, and multiple other entities may incur significant tangible start-up and recurring costs associated with MIDs and DDs. Increasingly, comprehensive responsibility-centered budgetary systems will require that these costs be calculated in program budgets. Further, MIDs and DDs may involve customized tuitions reflecting mutual in-kind contributions and the melding of differing tuition and fee systems. Thoroughly addressing such issues is critical to earning support for the financial aspects of proposals.

Indeed, consideration of such particulars must survive translation, discussion, and judgment through several overlapping layers of reviewers with varying perspectives. These include faculty senates, academic and resource planning offices, graduate college committees, visa procedure experts, budget offices, risk management professionals, and legal counsel, as previously noted. All the while, ongoing discussions will take place with the prospective partner institution.

For a variety of reasons, therefore, it is prudent for the large public institution to utilize a single campus office as the central coordinating actor in the degree collaboration process, from first contact with the faculty champion through advising the senior authority representing the proposal to institutional boards or state regulatory bodies for final approval. The office must be expert in the necessary procedures—and indeed should draft them. It should be empowered to bring parties together, to conduct negotiations internally and with the foreign partner(s), to provide leadership and facilitation in specialists' meetings as well as in policy discussions, and to retain responsibility for tracking the overall institutional process for advancing international degree collaborations. The process should be led by the senior international officer of the institution. Admittedly, title and location of such individuals will vary across universities and internationally.

Institutional partnerships spanning countries will generally bear the burden of establishing a high degree of mutual institutional confidence, often despite a lack of full familiarity with one another's institutional environments. Therefore, at least for some large public research universities in the United States, it is advisable that every effort be made to counter an often unstated uneasiness in the review process. This can be done with thorough information about accrediting body stances, the institutional standing, strength, track record in collaborations, and current partners of the proposed foreign collaborator(s), as well as a detailed and documented description of their regulatory environment and procedural requirements. Emphatically, the actual legal and institutional authority of the partner to confer an MID or a DD must be fully understood; specific wording, with or without supplementary documents, may depart from the diploma and degree nomenclature expected by the U.S. partner. The legal and institutional authority must be attested to in writing and be available as part of the institutional review process. Higher-level institutional support may hinge on this matter after other issues are resolved.

Ultimately, the question of confidence underlies all international collaborations. The ambitions of doctoral degree collaboration are less likely to be resisted when the partner institution is already a collaborator of long standing in a variety of frame-works, such as exchange agreements or consortium-based research collaborations. Institutional support is the result of a process conducted in a sound and stable frame-work. When the process is rigorous, and when the review framework is institution-ally engrained in the organizational system, support for well-conceived doctoral degree collaborations is to be expected from public research universities acting in the best interests of those they serve.

---

REFERENCES

Kirp, D.L. (2003). *Shakespeare, Einstein, and the bottom line: The marketing of higher education*. Cambridge: Harvard University Press.

Reinalda, B., & Kulesza, E. (2005). *The Bologna Process: Harmonizing Europe's higher education*. Bloomfield Hills, MI: Barbara Budrich Publishers.

Laying the Foundation – From Communication to Curriculum Design

# Vertical and Horizontal Communication in Transatlantic Degree Programs

By Jerome L. Neuner

## Framing the Problem

For any institution, developing a Transatlantic Degree Program (TDP) presents a series of layered and interconnected problems created by the many differences that exist between and among institutions. These include misaligned calendars, differential time to degrees, problems with student and faculty recruitment, multiple currency exchanges, credit transfer, external accreditations or ministry standards, articulation of course units and full degrees, and many others. This paper focuses on a somewhat narrower but still critical matter: once the initial degree program has been set up, at least on paper, what kind of continuing streams of communication both within an institution (vertical) and across the partner institutions (horizontal) need to be in place so that the program will meet with success on both sides of the Atlantic?

Most dual degrees originate as faculty-led initiatives. Faculty members are naturally enthusiastic about their fields of learning and their research. They see the potential for work with transatlantic colleagues and for students to have fascinating international learning experiences by studying abroad in a common or nearly common curriculum that is enriched because it brings a broader international perspective to the field.

Faculty members are embedded in institutions, and those institutions have set up their business and academic procedures in highly standardized ways to admit, enroll, register, charge fees, offer financial aid, orient, educate, evaluate, and award degrees. With a TDP in place, students arrive who are in a small, highly specialized dual or joint degree program that was possibly created in something of a "hothouse" or "skunkworks" environment of a few faculty members in perhaps four or fewer institutions, some of them in other countries. These new dual degree students are "non-standard" and are likely to require special attention at many steps through those standard processes. What are the best ways to make this a successful experience rather than one with many pitfalls?

## The Home Institution: A Vertical Review

As early as possible, even in the planning and drafting stage, offer campus officials a summary of the dual degree and ask for hidden issues or complications that may emerge as the dream program comes into reality. Using primarily American terminology, and in approximate order of importance, the list includes the following:

- **The Academic Officers**: The chair, dean, associate dean, and vice president (or equivalent officers) will have expert knowledge on such matters as the allowable waivers or substitutions in programs, special policies that may apply to your students such as "second degree" requirements, external accreditation or ministerial rules, corners that can and cannot be cut, potential conflicts in the demand for seats in required courses such as capstones, and many others.

- **The Registrar or Records Officer**: The person or office that finally decides who earns what degrees and when will want to know what special kinds of requests or orders he or she will be receiving. The program leaders will want to know how long it takes to produce records and deliver diplomas and degrees. A code in the system may be created to keep track of imports and exports of records in the program. Dual simultaneous enrollment may be required, as will credit transfers that reflect the agreement the partner institutions have made. These may conflict with existing procedures.

- **International Students Office**: Dual degree students should have a special orientation session describing the requirements and conditions of the program. This office also coordinates a number of vital concerns to which students must pay attention, such as health/life insurance, visas, immigration, ID cards, lodging, meals, public relations, taxpayer numbers (if employment is involved), and campus safety.

- **Student Accounts or Bursar**: Most dual degrees have some arrangement for student tuition or fee waivers. Without early warning, student accounts offices will normally charge every enrolled student full tuition and fees, so special students have to be handled individually. Any waivers will normally have to be accounted for in some budget and may spark an inquiry from the controller or other officials. If students are being paid mobility stipends, the situation is more complicated. Anything that goes on a student account will look like financial aid or a payment to the account. Refunds to students through the accounts office are a common way of paying mobility stipends. Finding out how this will be done in the home institution is vital. Most universities do not have routine procedures for simply giving money to students, even in programs that are fully funded by an outside source.

- **Internship Office**: In a number of fields such as engineering and business, the student internship—whether paid or unpaid—may be a central and fundamental part of the degree. Here again, the two sides may have conflicting versions. In the European model, the internship may be quite long and taken on as a full-time paid activity. In the U.S., an internship is frequently a summer activity or is part-time and completed in the academic term. Early communication with the office that handles these experiences will be required. There may also be visa implications for students who work in a country other than their own.

- **Sponsored Programs**: If external funding supports the TDP, specialists in managing this funding will be involved. In many institutions a pre-award expert reviews the budget, expected spending, regulations about allowable costs, matching expenses, and indirect costs. In some cases a post-award specialist explains how cash is managed, assists with reports, and helps by integrating funding into the ordinary financial operations of the institution. Every external grant is different, but each must be brought into basic functionality within the institution's systems.

- **Language Faculty**: If the program is going to bring an influx of students who are in serious need of language study, the language experts should be called in to discuss options such as pre-departure study at the home university, pre-semester immersion at the host university, language testing, and end-of-program proficiency exams.

- **Payroll**: If there are going to be stipends to visiting faculty or outside evaluators, a number of rules will come into play, including taxes, deductions, receipts, identity numbers, official addresses, and other concerns. Countries have different rules, and institutions have different procedures for all such transactions.

- **Public Relations**: A TDP is something to be boasted about as a valuable institutional achievement and attraction for students. Coverage in institutional or local media can help with finding new partners for sustainability and is a tribute to the people who have worked on the project. The PR office also connects to the institution's development and fundraising offices, who may want to present your activity to potential donors.

- **Designers and IT**: Many programs will want to have brochures, websites, online work spaces, videos, slide shows, web 2.0 communications, and course or program management capacity.

- **President/Rector**: He or she is not likely to have time for any aspect of the TDP, but signing an MOU or MOA is almost always required, and no better signature or stamp of approval exists.

## Abroad: The Horizontal Perspective

Ideally, everyone involved in a TPD would have an open channel to everyone else at all the partners. A more realistic and practical version is likely to emerge.

- **Academic Officers, Records Office, International Student Office:** This triad of counterparts is undoubtedly the most critical set of relationships. These three groups or individuals need not just a superficial but a deep grasp of the activity: the components of the degree articulation, the individual faculty and students involved, the final objectives, the funding realities, and the flow of information to other subordinate offices. On a day-to-day, semester-by-semester, and year-to-year basis these groups must continually inform their counterparts abroad and in the home country of the progress of the activity toward objectives, any problems that are occurring, deadlines, course unit offerings and schedules, special events, and general early warning of impending failure of any part of the activity. These groups will also gather all information and will compose the narrative that will go into reports to ministries or other funding sources, select students for the program, send and receive guest lecturers, and evaluate the program internally according to the institutions' standards. A failure of any one arm of the triad is likely to have immediate negative consequences including, in the worst case, complete loss of the program, loss of funding, and student failure to complete degrees. Good work among these groups leads to the successful full mainstreaming of the activity, even if the founders go on to other work. The basic tools of this exchange will be email lists, full access to joint project management software or programs, and the old-fashioned but still useful telephone.

- **Faculty:** In the typical case, the founders begin looking for new activities to initiate, and it is likely that colleagues in their discipline will carry on the original TDP. Peer faculty relationships are fostered by actual mobility, continuing communication, joint teaching and research, and possibly joint fundraising for new or extended activities. The reward systems for faculty vary from one institution to another, but the universals exist: faculty development, international perspective on the field of knowledge, creative teaching and course development, and the simple but rewarding pleasure of having interesting colleagues in distant places.

- **Others:** As a program comes through its early years, matures, is mainstreamed, and achieves a place of pride in the institutions, the service offices develop new routines to handle the exceptions, and eventually the exceptions cease to be exceptions. Along the way new and better business procedures may be developed, and the institution will become more adaptive to other sorts of changes as well. Initial stresses disappear. The whole institution is now better for the work of the pathfinders who first initiated the TDP. Other interesting partnerships will be easier to manage. New activities are more easily sustained. The institution grows and changes.

## Conclusion

International dual and joint degrees are a growing phenomenon in world higher education. They will become even more prominent as universities recognize that partnerships can improve teaching and learning and possibly save money, since one institution will not have to provide all the resources for a degree. Making TDPs happen is something of a tribute to the shared values of all higher education institutions: the love of learning, the desire for discovery, the hope for better societies. Higher education should serve as a good example to all the other forms of endeavor that occur internationally, such as trade, statecraft, relief work, and justice. Dual and joint degrees are worth the effort.

# Getting to Know You: Designing Joint Curricula and Fostering Sustained Communication among Partner Institutions

By Lori Thompson

Over the past decade, the State University of New York (SUNY) has developed partnerships with several universities abroad that have resulted in the establishment of dual diploma programs at the undergraduate and graduate levels. The largest system-wide initiative has involved nine universities in Turkey and nine SUNY partner institutions, enrolling more than 2,000 Turkish students in 27 programs since 2003. Of those students, nearly 500 have graduated as of summer 2009. Additional programs have begun with partners in Mexico, Russia, China, Azerbaijan, Poland, and other countries. Despite differences between programs in academic field, program structure, and partner university, several pragmatic strategies developed over multiple programs can be applied on a broad basis. The experiences of more than a dozen SUNY institutions have led to the implementation of many similar practices in each program.

In developing a program, the tasks of merging the curricula of partner institutions and satisfying general education or core curriculum requirements while maintaining the level of specialization required by both sides involve an investment of considerable time, repeated visits, and continued attention beyond the initial years of enrollment. A foundation to support these and other key elements of dual diploma programs must include an established routine of communication that is sustainable through changes in administration and faculty member participation.

## Designing Joint Curricula

### Program Structure

This discussion of program structure will focus on the SUNY/Turkey dual diploma programs, which currently enroll only Turkish students. The first 10 programs with Turkish partners were initiated in fields designated by a bilateral advisory board, which primarily included provosts, vice provosts for international education, and the equivalent vice rectors of Turkish universities. The advisory board selected curriculum committees to determine each program's structure and curriculum. The curriculum committees included faculty members from both sides and at least one person occupying an administrative role in each department or school/faculty.

It is important that the curriculum committees visit each partner institution's campus during the development process so that they can meet as many of their counterparts as possible, tour the institution, and meet students. During the course of examining, comparing, and discussing the curricula, general education requirements, residency requirements, course descriptions, and transfer credit issues, the ideal structure or pattern of study should emerge. In SUNY's programs, structure has been based upon many factors, such as:

- Lower and upper division courses are divided equally among the partners, avoiding traditional 2+2 models whenever possible.

- Curriculum committees should have the flexibility to create a structure that reflects the strengths of both partners and the unique needs of each academic program, rather than attempting to fit a program to a predetermined pattern. For example, a 1+2+1 model may be most useful for programs requiring a practical teaching experience or other internship in the home country.

- Online courses can be used when acceptable to both partners.

- Internship or Optional Practical Training (OPT) opportunities should be maximized for students. U.S. immigration law allows eligible students on F-1 visas to remain in the country for temporary employment, or OPT, in the student's field of study.

General Education

While extensive general education (GE) or core curriculum requirements are more common for U.S. higher education institutions, it is important to recognize the core curriculum requirements of both partners and to find ways to satisfy all requirements without placing additional burden on a merged curriculum that is most likely quite full. Even among U.S. universities, GE requirements for baccalaureate programs vary to a large degree. The SUNY general education program requires a minimum of 30 credits (roughly one year) to be completed before graduation. SUNY dual diploma programs have addressed GE in a variety of ways:

- Creation of a dual diploma academic policies committee at the U.S. institution to address GE issues that are specific to dual diploma programs.

- Students coming to the U.S. institution from a country in which English is not the official language may be exempt from the foreign language GE requirement. This exemption may depend on whether or not courses in the local language are required in the joint curriculum.

- Utilization of credit toward an International Baccalaureate (IB) diploma to satisfy some GE requirements.

- Creation of a mechanism for the regular submission and consideration of new courses offered by the non-U.S. partner university for GE credit.

- Circulation of course selection surveys to students prior to semesters spent at the U.S. partner campus, designating which available courses satisfy particular GE requirements.

Academic Policies

Dual diploma students, like all students, are subject to the academic policies of the university at which they are in residence. When students move back and forth, sometimes alternating years at each partner institution, this rule should be clearly stated. Partner universities should have an understanding of each others' regular academic policies and should agree on the rules that are specific to the dual diploma programs. It is important for each partner to issue a special academic policies document to address the unique issues resulting from the dual diploma partnership, such as those described in the examples below.

- Academic policies should include:

    - Rules for good academic standing

    - Guidelines for probation, dismissal, withdrawal

    - Grade calculation: quality points and letter grades

    - Repeating courses, grade replacement policy, role in GPA calculation

    - Issues regarding prerequisite courses

    - Academic integrity

    - Appeals process

    - Other issues as needed from the university's overall academic policy

- What grade constitutes a course failure? Course failure may vary between partner institutions and should be made clear among partners and to students. Sufficient opportunities for retaking courses should be available, including summer and winter sessions, as available, and online courses, as agreed by both partners.

- When students perform satisfactorily at one partner but not at the other, what are the rules for dismissal? In the SUNY/Turkey programs, a dismissal by one partner constitutes a dismissal from the entire program. The partners should also discuss readmission policies.

- How is the cumulative GPA calculated? In most programs, separate GPAs are calculated by each partner university. Upon graduation, students receive a transcript from each partner.

Special Curriculum Issues – Examples in Practice

- Curricula are continually revisited, and sufficient flexibility is maintained to allow changes to be made as new issues arise. Even after six years, the SUNY/Turkey programs require adjustments as changes occur at the partner institutions and as unique situations arise with students.

- SUNY institutions have devised new or additional academic success workshops. The workshops address certain needs that have risen to the attention of faculty and coordinators by virtue of having significant cohorts of students from a particular country or region.

- In certain areas, such as global and international affairs, students have needed supplemental instruction focused on American history and politics. Faculty members have designed an online course administered during the semester prior to students' arrival on campus and a team-taught, one-day session during orientation.

- One campus added a new course based on the successful College Life and Social Issues class offered to first-year students. The course was adapted for a cross-cultural audience and offered as part of the residential life experience. Topics include diversity, relationships, academic expectations, and dealing with conflict.

- When curricula are heavy with prerequisites and credits per semester, such as SUNY programs in marine engineering and maritime transportation, two curriculum models are available to prevent high numbers of students from falling behind schedule. One model plans for students to arrive in the spring semester of the first year, and the alternative allows students an additional semester in Turkey.

## Designing a Coordination and Communication Structure

While communication and networking technologies have brought unprecedented opportunities to communicate across the street and across the world, it remains critical to work with partners on a face-to-face basis. An exchange of visits is important at the outset, but face-to-face communication must be maintained to ensure academic quality and to properly administer the programs. One might imagine that a basic forum such as a listserv would provide supplemental communication. In the SUNY/Turkey program, the established listserv is used not at all.

The bilateral structure of coordination for most of the SUNY dual diploma programs is similar to that of the SUNY/Turkey program:

- **Campus Coordinator:** A vice president or vice rector, usually the provost or vice rector of academic or student affairs. Oversees all dual diploma programs at the institution, handles important academic policy issues and financial matters, and works with program coordinators.

- **Program Coordinator:** Lead faculty member, sometimes a department head or dean. Handles or directs academic student advising, academic issues with counterparts, curriculum changes, and so forth. At least one program coordinator is essential for each dual diploma field.

- **Administrative Coordinator:** Responsible for all nonacademic coordination, but may work with the program coordinators on academic issues. Reports directly to the campus coordinator and works with many offices on campus, including international student and scholar services, registrar, housing, student accounts, counseling and career services, and so forth.

- **Dual diploma program offices:** Established at several of the partner institutions on both sides. The office is usually directed by the administrative coordinator and includes one or two assistants.

The coordination structure must be supported by a schedule of face-to-face meetings. Opportunities for direct communication are fostered in a number of ways, such as those described below.

- **Annual bilateral meeting of all coordinators:** Coordinators meet alternately in each country and have separate meetings at their partner institutions during the days before or after the main meeting. The meetings provide opportunities for coordinators to address specific curricular and student issues and to meet with students at their home institution.

- **Annual meeting of coordinators on each side:** Three to four months prior to the bilateral meeting, each side convenes all coordinators to address internal issues and to prepare for the bilateral gathering.

- **Faculty exchange:** Faculty members often accompany groups of students for the initial weeks of the first semester at the partner institution. If possible, faculty members remain for the semester to teach courses in the program and undertake joint research with their counterparts. Utilizing the Fulbright program or other sources of external funds to support faculty exchange is strongly encouraged.

- **Established practices for transcript sharing:** To facilitate proper academic advising, particularly for students who move back and forth each year, coordinators must establish a mechanism for the timely sharing of student transcripts.

- **University administration involvement:** Communication between the presidents and rectors of partner institutions should occur at least annually, if not more frequently. Campus coordinators should arrange presidential visits to partner institutions on an annual basis and as soon as possible after a change in administration. Graduation events provide good opportunities for such visits.

- **Coordinator visits for on-site orientation:** The regular international student orientation should be supplemented by one or two additional predeparture orientation sessions in the home country. A welcome orientation during the first semester of enrollment in the home country, conducted by the partner's administrative or program coordinators, helps students to feel that they are truly dual-enrolled. A second session provides predeparture information, course registration and housing details, and information about visa procedures.

- **Events:** The diplomatic representations of both partner countries are invited to special university events (student fashion shows and graduation ceremonies, to name a few). Expatriate and alumni associations can be very helpful in organizing or hosting local gatherings and speaking events. Local political officials and legislators may also be invited to these events.

- **External communication:** Focus groups have been created during the annual bilateral meeting to work on outreach to external sources of scholarship support. Coordinators have also secured direct funding from businesses. For example, the maritime industry in Istanbul provided scholarships for the top students in the SUNY/Turkey marine engineering and maritime transportation programs.

- **Embassies and consulates:** Coordinators should be in contact with the embassies and consulates in their partner countries to provide program information and to inquire about ways to prepare students for visa application processes. Consular officers or others responsible for issuing visas rotate to new posts every few years, so outreach should be ongoing.

# Transatlantic Degree Program – At a Glance

| | |
|---|---|
| Name of Program | Dual Diploma Programs between the State University of New York and Turkish Universities |
| Partner Institutions | Turkish universities:<br><br>Anadolu University<br>Bilkent University<br>Boğaziçi University<br>Ege University<br>Hacettepe University<br>Işık University<br>Istanbul Technical University<br>Izmir University of Economics<br>Middle East Technical University<br><br>SUNY institutions:<br><br>Binghamton University<br>SUNY Brockport<br>University at Buffalo<br>SUNY Cortland<br>Empire State College<br>Fashion Institute of Technology<br>SUNY Fredonia<br>SUNY Geneseo<br>Maritime College<br>SUNY New Paltz |
| Location of Study | Students spend approximately half of their studies at a Turkish university and half at a partner SUNY campus; structure varies by program |
| Academic Field(s) | Business (undergraduate and MBA), civil engineering, computer science, economics, environmental engineering, fashion design, global and international affairs, information systems engineering, international relations, marine engineering, maritime transportation management, public relations, software engineering, teaching English to speakers of other languages, textile development and marketing |
| Academic Level | 27 undergraduate programs, 1 graduate program |

| Year Started | 2003 | What type of degree is awarded? | Double |
|---|---|---|---|

| Language(s) of Instruction | English |
|---|---|

**How many students participated in the most recent year of the program?**

| | Turkish students | 1,794 | U.S. students | 0 | Other students | 0 |
|---|---|---|---|---|---|---|

**How many students have graduated from the program since it began?**

| | Turkish students | 483 | U.S. students | 0 | Other students | 0 |
|---|---|---|---|---|---|---|

# Curriculum Design for Joint Master's Programs: Challenges and Opportunities

By Ulla Kriebernegg and Roberta Maierhofer

Curriculum design is one of the most challenging components of joint program development. Although issues like legal requirements, funding, student and faculty mobility, institutional support, and quality assurance are by no means less demanding, the curriculum is at the core of a joint degree program. Developing it requires intensive collaboration between academics and administrators from all partner universities. As the curriculum is usually based on existing courses, the challenge is to put together a cohesive joint curriculum while respecting the offerings and focus areas of the individual universities involved.

This article is a summary of best practice examples regarding joint curriculum development gathered during the past six years of intensive work in the field of transatlantic program development. Since 2003, the University of Graz has been the coordinating university for the development and implementation of six interdisciplinary joint degree programs at the master's level. We are referring to "joint degree programs" according to the following definition: "Students study at (at least) two higher education institutions and receive upon completion of the study program a single degree certificate issued and signed by all the participating institutions jointly" (Obst & Kuder, 2009). The programs coordinated by the University of Graz (for further information refer to the Graz project website at www.jointdegree.eu) are in line with the Bologna accords and share the following characteristics:

- The programs are research-based master's programs (120 European Credit Transfer and Accumulation System or ECTS units, two years).

- The study programs, curricula, admission, and examination regulations are jointly developed and recognized by all consortium partners, while respecting the individual universities' conditions.

- Students spend part of their studies (minimum 30 ECTS credits, one semester) at another partner institution. These credits, as well as all examinations completed at a partner institution, are fully and automatically recognized at a student's home institution.

- The courses offered are taken from the already existing programs of the participating universities. No new courses need to be developed. Each university contributes its own field of expertise to the program.

- Summer schools serve as "catch-up classes" or bridge courses that count toward the 30 ECTS credit requirement of the mobility phase.

- Upon successful completion of the study program, students receive one joint diploma that is issued and recognized by all partner institutions.

Needless to say, not all of the challenges and problems that arise when trying to plan and implement joint programs among highly diverse institutions have been resolved, or even charted. Despite the ongoing structural harmonization of European systems, each university in each country still has its specific issues, and when setting out to develop a joint program, one quickly learns that "the devil is in the details." Therefore, it is impossible to come up with general guidelines or instructions for joint curriculum development. There are, however, some basic (and not so basic) recommendations that should be considered for a successful program development. Among these are the "10 Golden Rules for New Joint Master's Programs" (European University Association, 2004) that need to be mentioned when planning to develop a joint program. Although these rules are very simple, they include the main issues that become relevant during the development phase.

It is often assumed that the Bologna process has made it simpler to develop joint curricula within Europe and that including American partners in the project can be quite challenging. Our experience, however, showed that this is not the case. Regarding structural differences in curriculum design, such as non-European grading schemes, for example, U.S. universities have proven far more flexible than their European counterparts. In our project, the modular system of the curriculum was designed to accommodate the needs of a U.S. university (in this case, the City College of the City University of New York), which was easier than expected due to the way U.S. universities function in terms of program development and independence. A conversion table for ECTS grades and U.S. grades was added to the cooperation contract, the second key document that complements the curriculum, thereby allowing the consortium to also incorporate universities that are not using ECTS credits.

Another important tool worth mentioning in this context is the "Tuning Project" (European Commission—Education and Training), an EU-funded project that was started in 2000 to harmonize European educational structures with emphasis on the "subject area level," that is, the content of studies. It provided excellent advice regarding curriculum modularization. In order to reconcile the partner universities' different curricula, a modular structure with a clear emphasis on learning outcomes instead of detailed academic contents emerged as the perfect solution to accommodate each partner's needs.

In the case of the Graz projects, it was stipulated that the joint programs tap into already existing programs and course offerings. The consortium members decided that the added value would be a larger variety of courses students could choose from and a range of dedicated professors with diverse areas of research who could act as their teachers and advisors. No extra courses needed to be either implemented or, more importantly, funded.

However, before such decisions were made, a lot of small steps had to be taken. Sometimes, "two steps forward, one step back" was the order of the day. Therefore, stamina may be a key qualification when setting out to develop a joint program. Especially at the beginning, when the coordinators met for the first time and differing expectations were difficult to reconcile, it was vital for coordinators to possess social and cross-cultural competence paired with detailed background knowledge of the subject matter, regarding both academic and administrative issues. Building a trustworthy relationship is central when it comes to negotiating a basic framework and creating a joint vision—which are crucial for the sustainability of a program. Developing a common understanding of the academic contents means discussing and balancing different assumptions and interpretations, harmonizing them, and translating these into time frames and work packages. Ideally, these efforts will, upon completion, lead to a curriculum that meets or even exceeds each university's expectations.

Apart from establishing good personal relationships, it is strategically important to enhance the project's visibility at the university hosting the meetings; e.g., by inviting deans, provosts, students, and fellow department members to at least parts of the meetings (like lunch breaks or dinners). Raising interest contributes to the commitment of the institution and thus makes a program more sustainable.

In addition to academic aspects, curricular issues always involve various administrative levels. A thorough project environment analysis of financial matters, credits allocation, and other coordination processes needs to be carried out, in view of these curricular concerns. Thus, one issue that needs to be addressed right at the beginning is the schedule of responsibilities for implementing new curricula at each university. While in some countries, universities are autonomous and can make such decisions themselves, universities in other countries may have to apply to ministries and are dependent on national or regional developments. However, it is crucial to keep track of the individual stages of such decision-making processes in a transparent way. In the Graz case, it proved of great advantage to have administrative support sufficient to coordinate the flow of information among the partner universities as well as to provide information on national and regional legal systems to the consortium partners. This implies that academics and administrators have to work together regarding the successful completion of a joint curriculum.

As these examples show, a solid knowledge of legal requirements and structural processes is necessary for the coordinating team in order to reconcile the very different needs of the several partner institutions when developing a joint curriculum. Within our projects, university management had to adapt statutes or bylaws, including passages referring to joint degree programs. More importantly, however, the consortium members worked on the basic assumption that each involved university maintained high standards of teaching and research, had good quality assurance mechanisms in place, and operated on a sophisticated level concerning regulations and procedures. Having chosen the partner institutions carefully, the negotiations were conducted on the basis of mutual trust, and joint regulations were kept to a minimum. As a rule, the respective regulations of each individual university guarantee a high standard in teaching and research. In addition, however, joint quality assurance mechanisms were developed, and accreditation processes required by partner institutions and by European agencies were set up as part of the program; for example, in the case of German universities, the Accreditation, Certification, and Quality Assurance Institute (see website: http://acquin.org/en/index.php) and Agentur für Qualitätssicherung durch Akkreditierung von Studiengängen (see website: www.aqas.de).

Regardless of the challenges of development and implementation that such joint degree programs face, they are definitely worth all necessary efforts. Once the joint degree program has been launched and has become part of the university's standard program offerings, all headaches are forgotten, and we can offer our students a truly international program that reflects the strengths of all of the universities involved. Coordinating several joint programs not only contributes to a university's international reputation but also creates a global network of administrators, scholars, and students who share common goals. It facilitates international mobility and advances the implementation of Bologna goals. It increases campus internationalization and cross-cultural awareness. Despite the challenges such an attempt entails, the joint degree projects described in this article have always been considered worthwhile undertakings by everybody involved.

REFERENCES

European University Association (EUA). (2004). *Developing joint masters programmes in Europe: Results of the EUA Joint Masters Project. January 2002 - March 2004.* Brussels: Ed. European University Association (EUA). Accessed March 10, 2009 from www.eua.be/eua/jsp/en/upload/Joint_Masters_report.1087219975578.pdf.

Obst, D. & Kuder, M. (2009). *Joint and double degree programs in the transatlantic context: A Survey Report.* New York: Institute of International Education. Accessed August 24, 2009 from www.iienetwork.org/page/TDP/.

## Transatlantic Degree Program – At a Glance

| | |
|---|---|
| Name of Program | European Joint Master's Degree in English and American Studies |
| Partner Institutions | Karl-Franzens-University of Graz, Austria<br>Otto-Friedrich-University Bamberg, Germany<br>Ca'Foscari University Venice, Italy<br>University of Pecs, Hungary<br>City College of the City University of New York, U.S.<br>Roehampton University London, UK<br>Paris Diderot, France |
| Location of Study | See above |
| Academic Field(s) | Linguistics, Literary Studies, Cultural Studies |
| Academic Level | Graduate (MA) |

| Year Started | 2007 | What type of degree is awarded? | Joint |
|---|---|---|---|

| Language(s) of Instruction | English |
|---|---|

How many students participated in the most recent year of the program?

| | EU students | 7 | U.S. students | 3 | Other students | 4 |
|---|---|---|---|---|---|---|

How many students have graduated from the program since it began?

| | EU students | 0 | U.S. students | 0 | Other students | 0 |
|---|---|---|---|---|---|---|

Putting Programs into Practice

# Training Lawyers for Transnational Practice: Building Dual Degree Programs in Law

By Macarena Sáez and Jamie Welling

Six years ago, the American University Washington College of Law (WCL) began an ambitious project: to train lawyers who would be capable of practicing locally in two different countries. The project was broader than creating just one dual degree program with one country; it aimed to create opportunities in multiple countries at the same time. The goal was to establish conditions that would allow students from various countries, including the U.S., to be able to practice as a "domestic" lawyer both at home and abroad. Today, WCL offers international Juris Doctor (JD) dual degree programs where students earn their U.S. law degree (JD) and the equivalent law degree from universities in Canada, France, Spain, and Australia. Presently, WCL is exploring the development of similar models with countries such as Mexico and the United Kingdom. The programs have presented new opportunities for lawyers to go beyond taking classes based on international law concepts and instead take this knowledge to a new and more intense level as transnational lawyers.

As difficult as it is to establish any dual degree program, implementing international JD dual degree programs has further complications. This is particularly true given the consideration of local structures of legal systems and law programs lasting up to five years in most countries. Establishing international dual degrees requires attention to details not necessarily apparent from the start. Despite the challenges, WCL has found the results to be worth the effort.

There are several important areas to consider when developing an international dual degree program. Due to the fact that each institution is unique, we will only briefly touch upon three key areas WCL has found to be important for our programs: choosing a partner institution, deciding on the number of students to involve, and developing a four-year program that must combine external programs lasting between three and five years, while maintaining the substantive curriculum of each place.

## Choosing a Partner Institution

It is extremely important for an institution to have clear objectives in place for implementing a dual degree program prior to choosing the specific partner institution. There are many reasons why schools decide to offer dual degree options; for instance, some institutions may have a strong desire to associate their name with a particular foreign university for the purposes of recruiting or marketing. While these goals may be legitimate, they may lead to programs that are unworkable or add little value to the degrees individually earned.

WCL's international JD dual degree programs are very complex because of the strict legal practice regulations that exist in the U.S. and most other countries. For instance, some countries do not allow foreign nationals to practice law, while some countries have very strict rules for taking the bar exam and may only allow 20-25 percent of their own domestic graduates to sit for the exam or even practice law. In addition to the law degree, some countries have additional requirements for practice after graduation, such as apprenticeships that may take one or two years to complete. Although these are only examples of some of the complications that make JD dual degree programs so difficult to implement, they illustrate the need to make the selection process of the partner institution an instrumental factor in the ultimate success of the programs.

Before deciding to create a dual degree program with a particular institution and country, we suggest taking the following steps:

### Research the Professional Practice Guidelines

It is important to do a thorough study of the professional practice regulations of the country where the partnership will take place. Relying on the information given by the potential foreign institution may not be sufficient, especially in the case of disciplines such as law, the regulation of which, in many countries, is not in the hands of the universities or the Department of Education. The information provided by the potential partner institution may not be regarded as "official." In many cases, although the counterpart institution may be well intentioned, it may have never looked at the professional practice guidelines and/or the process very closely, especially with regard to foreign nationals. Additionally, sometimes the process of obtaining a license to practice a profession in the host country may not be complex, but it may require the payment of high fees and the presentation of forms and documents. A process like this may seem easy on paper, but it may be a nightmare in practice. Inquire about detailed information on this process, such as how long it will take to complete, how much it will cost, what it will mean to present "official translations" of transcripts, where a foreigner may obtain criminal records in the country, and other such questions.

## Research the School Environment and Available Support Systems

Understanding the environment of the potential partner is very important for the development and success of the program. One of the major obstacles that dual degree programs face between American graduate programs and foreign programs is the difference between graduate and undergraduate education. For example, in many countries, there is no system of undergraduate education comparable to that in the U.S.; therefore, U.S. law students generally have completed a four-year degree and tend to be older. Programs aimed at obtaining two professional degrees will usually involve interaction between the older American students, who have at least 5 years of education (4 years of undergraduate education plus at least one year of a master's or JD degree), and younger foreign students (for example, where the time in law school is equivalent to the time a student spends completing a bachelor's degree in the U.S.) who have recently graduated from high school. For U.S. institutions, it is important to know if their potential partners host a large body of foreign students, not only for the benefits of diversity, but because they tend to be older and at a similar stage in life, which can benefit the participating students.

At the same time, schools looking to partner with institutions in the U.S. should also seek institutions that have a diverse student body and an institutionalized support system for foreign students. The use of the Socratic method to teach law may be very different from what foreign students are used to, and many students will be significantly younger and sometimes less experienced than their peers. The teaching methodology at the master's or JD level in the U.S. can be very intense, and the environment can be highly competitive, which can make it more of a struggle to succeed. Having a reliable program in place staffed with people who are aware of these dynamics will provide important support to students, from academic and professional advising to visa information.

## Research Curricula and Teaching Methodology of the Institution

It is important to understand the differences in programs of study and teaching methodology before making a decision on partnering for a dual degree program. In the case of law programs this is especially important. Countries embedded in the Continental legal tradition tend to have more rigid curricula than U.S. institutions. Finding equivalencies in the schools' curricula can be rather challenging. In this sense, it is important to look for institutions willing to be as flexible as possible and with faculty that share the goals set forth by both institutions.

## Deciding on the Number of Students to Participate in the Program

While this question is left to the individual school, our experience over the past few years has resulted in WCL's decision to purposely keep the number low of students allowed to participate in the international JD dual degree program. Each of the four country programs we have only accepts up to four students to participate each year

(16 total) and only receives the same number from each partner. Some of the reasons for the lower participant numbers include:

## Calculating Tuition Costs

In the case of WCL's international JD dual degree programs, the program works similarly to semester exchange programs, where each student pays tuition to the home institution and no tuition is paid to the host institution. It is possible to maintain this tuition balance when fewer students are selected to participate, in order to avoid one school sending more than another. Graduate students from U.S. institutions tend to travel in much lower numbers than students from institutions in other regions of the world, such as Europe. If only a few students are expected to travel per year, it will be simpler to keep this tuition balance even.

## Unforeseen Issues

During the first years of the program, regardless of how well planned it is, there will be issues that were not apparent during the planning phase. For example, issues may arise regarding scheduling, participation in selective journals and groups, participant illness, or graduation. Participants in graduate dual degree programs often require additional, more individualized support, which can be more intensive from an administrative perspective. Therefore, the implementation of an international dual degree program is a complex operation that requires a great deal of coordination, communication, and good will between the two institutions. Although a program may require the participation of only two schools, there will be other internal departments of both universities involved as well. A successful program requires the participation of many offices such as the academic units involved (law schools in our case), international student offices, registrar's office, and office of the provost and/or president, to name a few. These offices must be aware of the policy and procedures of the program. All this coordination takes place internally but also collaboratively with the programs overseas, usually involving communication with people who do not speak the same language or have the same type of work environment and responsibilities. Having smaller numbers of students participating in the program has eased the coordination problems and enabled WCL to promptly resolve any issues with its partners.

## The Possibility for Real Immersion

International dual degree programs should not be viewed and treated as regular study abroad opportunities and for that reason should be kept small, providing an incentive for students to interact and ultimately become local students themselves. The goal of the WCL programs is to train foreign students as local attorneys, so they can practice in two or more countries. Sometimes fulfilling this goal requires a student to possess skills that can only be truly absorbed through experiencing the daily life of the country where they are studying, such as the ability to communicate in a different language and understand certain aspects of a foreign culture. It is tempting to think of programs in which 10 or 30 students participate together in a program organized by their home institution, but located in a foreign country. From our experience, when many students travel together, especially in larger numbers, they tend to live together, socialize primarily among themselves, and study together. While a large number of students can create a good support network for those involved, remaining in classes surrounded by peers from home or other exchange students may also impede the experience. While this approach meets the goals of some universities and students, this type of environment neglects a fundamental element of the dual degree program by discouraging the student from becoming fully immersed in the local traditions, customs, and language.

## Combining Diverse University Programs while Maintaining the Substantive Curriculum of Each School

The most important and challenging part of establishing an international dual degree program is the development of program curricula. One of the advantages of dual degree programs for students is that they allow students to obtain two degrees in a reduced amount of time. It is therefore instrumental to make sure the concentrated curriculum agreed upon by both partners gives students substantive knowledge of the subject, meets all national requirements (e.g., American Bar Association), but determines what classes may be waived in order to provide a time reduction for the completion of both degrees. For WCL, it has been highly advantageous to have the program of study fully determined at the partner university, especially prior to sending any students abroad.

When the dual degree is set up at the master's level, the difference in the length of each program may not create a significant challenge. Most programs will last between one and two years, and some classes will cover the same areas in each program. In the case of degrees that are treated as undergraduate education in some countries and graduate education in others, the structure of the curriculum will require more thought. Law degrees in Europe, for instance, may normally take between four and five years to complete. Law degrees in the U.S., on the other hand, may take three years to complete. In Europe, the curriculum may be more rigid, with few elective classes. In the U.S., the program of study may be more flexible, with fewer mandatory classes to complete and more electives.

These differences pose a challenge when combining two programs. WCL has been successful at finding adequate compromises for the students participating in the programs. For instance, given that American students in graduate programs have already completed a four-year undergraduate degree and are usually older than students in similar programs in other regions of the world, some classes are able to be waived by the host institution or students have been able to take classes as an independent study along with their regular course load. While solutions like this can work very well, it is imperative that students participate in at least half of their classes with regular degree students from the host institution.

## Final Thoughts

Developing an international dual degree program involves a great deal of communication and coordination between institutions that have the flexibility to design a program that best meets the needs of both partners and participating students. The planning phase of such a program should not be rushed, and program administrators should collect as much research and feedback as possible before diving into the process. Nevertheless, over the years WCL has experienced a growing number of prospective and current law students interested in becoming lawyers both at home and abroad, and many of our program alumni have continued to stay and practice in the country where they completed their additional degree. While the three points elaborated in this article are not the only aspects to consider when developing an effective dual degree program, we hope they will provide a springboard for continued thought, dialogue, and exploration.

# Transatlantic Degree Program – At a Glance

| Name of Program | International JD Dual Degree Program | | | | | |
|---|---|---|---|---|---|---|
| Partner Institutions | American University Washington College of Law University Carlos III (Spain) University of Paris X—Nanterre (France) | | | | | |
| Location of Study | 2 Years in the U.S., 2 years in Spain or France | | | | | |
| Academic Field(s) | Law | | | | | |
| Academic Level | Law—J.D. equivalent | | | | | |
| Year Started | | What type of degree is awarded? | | Double | | |
| Language(s) of Instruction | | English, French, Spanish | | | | |
| How many students participated in the most recent year of the program? | | | | | | |
| | EU students | 7 | U.S. students | 10 | Other students | 7 |
| How many students have graduated from the program since it began? | | | | | | |
| | EU students | 8 | U.S. students | 20 | Other students | 11 |

# Confronting European Experience with American Realities: How Columbia University is Setting Up a Dual Civil Engineering Master's Degree with the University of Bologna

By Régine Lambrech

Dual degree programs have been part of the higher education landscape in Europe since the 1970s. During her 19 years of affiliation with a French grande école, the author helped to set up dual engineering degrees with higher education institutions that were members of the TIME (Top Industrial Managers for Europe) network. Students could choose to obtain a dual degree at any one of the 34 different member institutions (there are now 52 members). That meant spending two years at the host institution studying engineering courses in the language of the host institution, adding only one additional year to the length of study necessary to obtain the regular engineering degree at the home institution. By the year 2000, approximately 10 percent of the graduating class of 300 students was enrolled for a dual degree. Students had begun to choose to study with us because of our extensive study abroad options.

Setting up these dual degrees was labor-intensive, but the benefits for our students were clear: graduates had engineering qualifications that were recognized in two countries, and they had significant experience being immersed in two cultural, learning, and even working environments. Multinational companies constantly came to us seeking direct recruiting access to the students enrolled in the dual degree programs—on average, five months before the students were scheduled to graduate. In fact, a June 14, 2001 report on Expatriation of Competencies, Capital and Companies (see www.senat.fr/rap/r00-386/r00-386.html) that was presented to the French Senate states that 42 percent of French dual degree engineers obtain their first job in another country, and for half of those graduates, the job is for a foreign company. Furthermore, it states that 35 percent of the foreign dual degree graduates work in France and that 53 percent of the dual degree graduates (three-quarters of the French graduates and one-third of the foreign graduates) work in French companies, whether in France or in another country. This is a testament to the success of the dual degree programs.

Now employed at Columbia University in the city of New York, the author is using her European dual degree experience to work with engineering professors to establish dual degrees: a BS/MS with the Ecole Polytechnique in France, and an MS/Laurea Magistrale with the University of Bologna, which is the subject of this article. Some of the challenges are the same (e.g., establishing course and grading system equivalencies, assuring sustainability, making accommodations so that the program will work), but others have arisen because of the different educational arena here in the U.S.

It is no surprise to those familiar with the Bologna Declaration (signed in the Italian city of Bologna on June 19, 1999, by ministers in charge of higher education from 29 European countries) that professors from the University of Bologna would be the catalysts for the establishment of a dual master's degree program with Columbia. The logical contact here is a professor, originally from Italy, who has collaborated for a number of years with colleagues in civil engineering at the University of Bologna. Professor Raimondo Betti's inside knowledge of the Italian system of education, as well as the research areas of his colleagues at Bologna and his experience with the education policy and procedures here at Columbia, make him the perfect bridge between the two very different administrative, educational, and cultural systems.

Fully aware of the challenges that await us as we begin final preparations for this dual degree program, we decided to limit the numbers of participants to a maximum of 10. It is a well-known fact that American students prefer short-term study abroad periods and up until now have been less inclined to seek foreign degrees—even those taught entirely in English, which eliminate the need to be fluent speakers of the host country's language. Consequently, finding students willing to pay for and spend a full academic year at Bologna in addition to their master's degree here at Columbia will not be as easy for us as it will be for our Italian partners to find candidates to obtain a master's here at Columbia in addition to their degree from Bologna. In fact, the University of Bologna and other Italian universities have been sending us master's students for a number of years already, and we know that the Italian students recognize the benefit of the Columbia master's degree. Dual degrees are much more firmly established in the student mindset in Europe and are definitely not a hard sell. American students, however, tend to think that their American degree is enough to guarantee them a lifetime of employment. The current economic situation and massive layoffs will more than likely help persuade these students that they will have an advantage in the competition if they possess engineering qualifications in two countries. As a result, we are marketing this to the students as a further asset in their job search, and we are concurrently marketing the future dual degree graduates to Italian and American firms that each operate at home and/or in the other country. We believe, as is shown by the French study mentioned above, that students will quickly see the advantages of the dual degree when they are persuaded that it opens more doors on the job market, and we feel confident that future statistics will bear this out.

In setting this up, Columbia faced one big challenge that most American universities will confront when dealing with European partner institutions: the difference in fee structure between the two institutions. Bologna's tuition is about 3,000 euros (less than $5,000 at the time of this writing) while Columbia's is $34,000! Since most of the Italian students who come to Columbia will have some sort of external funding (scholarships, fellowships, corporate sponsorships), and because very few scholarships exist for American students wanting to do graduate studies abroad, we have agreed that each university will charge its own tuition and fees. If more than ten students are enrolled in the dual degree program in a single year, we will jointly agree on a special discount.

Our dual degree program is structured so that students are required to complete all requirements for the master's degree at both institutions. The University of Bologna even stipulates that its students will not receive their degree from Bologna if they do not receive the degree from Columbia. For legal reasons, Columbia cannot impose this same requirement on its students. What we have done is to work out a study plan for the students that will enable them to further specialize at the partner institution, thereby not retaking the same courses overseas but filling in the gaps in their first master's degree. In fact, it can also generally be said that Columbia's degree is more theoretical in nature, and Bologna's degree is of a more applied nature. At Bologna, the degree requires 60 credits of coursework (usually completed over two years) while Columbia's degree requires only 30 credits (usually completed over two semesters).

In practice, this dual degree means that Bologna students can spend one of their two years of study at Columbia and that Columbia students can obtain their Columbia degree, then spend an additional year at Bologna and obtain their second master's degree from Bologna. Columbia delivers a master's degree with an option to present a written thesis, while Bologna's Laurea Magistrale has a mandatory thesis requirement. Students who have completed 30 credits of coursework at Columbia may then apply to the University of Bologna and, if admitted, transfer those 30 credits and apply them to the 60 credits (120 European Credit Transfer and Accumulation System [ECTS] credits) required to obtain a Laurea Magistrale from Bologna. Bologna students can complete one year (or the equivalent of 30 American credits) and then come to Columbia to take 10 courses (30 credits), of which some may be thesis research work. They will then return to Bologna to defend their thesis research and afterwards receive both the Columbia Master's Degree in Civil Engineering and the Laurea Magistrale in Ingegneria Civile. This guarantees that all participants have a significant research element to their degrees, which they would not necessarily have had with the Columbia degree alone.

All students participating in this dual degree arrangement must satisfy the normal entrance requirements of both universities. For the purposes of helping admissions officers understand the grading system of the partner institution, the following grade equivalency table has been established:

TABLE 1: GRADE EQUIVALENCY TABLE

| Grades at Columbia University | Grades at the University of Bologna |
|---|---|
| A+ | 30L |
| A | 30 |
| A- | 28 |
| B+ | 26 |
| B | 25 |
| B- | 24 |
| C+ | 23 |
| C | 22 |
| C- | 21 |
| D+ | 20 |
| D | 19 |
| D- | 18 |
| F | respinto |

This table is to be used only for admissions guidelines and not transfer credits. Once either Bologna or Columbia students obtain the Columbia master's degree, those 30 credits automatically transfer as a package to the University of Bologna to be applied to the Laurea Magistrale. The grade equivalency table guarantees that admissions officers at both institutions will be able to make independent decisions to allow their admissions standards to remain high.

These are only a few of the issues we have dealt with in setting up this dual degree program. The true measures of the success of setting up dual degree programs are both the degree of good will that accompanies the discussions and, above all, the flexibility adopted by both sides in order to make concessions that will allow the program to work. When all is said and done, it is just as important for the professors who are negotiating these dual degrees to be flexible as is it to expect the student participants to be flexible. The commitment on both sides of the table was evident in our discussions, and this sometimes led us to bend rules in order to create a workable plan. The end result is a manageable and highly workable dual degree program that is a win-win for students and faculty at both universities.

Putting Programs into Practice

# Overcoming Challenges of Student Selection in Double Degree Cooperation

By Vuokko Iinatti and Tuija Mainela

Oulu Business School of the University of Oulu in Finland and the Bryan School of Business of the University of North Carolina at Greensboro (UNCG) have about three years of experience in double degree cooperation. In the following article, we describe the background and contents of the cooperation and then focus on the student selection process in the Oulu Business School. This issue has been seen as one of the major challenges of cooperation from the viewpoint of the Oulu Business School.

## Short Description of the Double Degree Cooperation

The Oulu Business School offers its master's-level students the possibility to complete a U.S. Master in Business Administration (MBA) degree by studying one year in the Bryan School of Business at UNCG. Two students with a bachelor's degree from the Oulu Business School are chosen to attend UNCG to study MBA courses for one academic year. The Bryan School of Business is committed to transferring half a year of master's-level studies at the Oulu Business School to their MBA degree. Similarly, the Oulu Business School is committed to transferring half a year of MBA studies to its Master of Science degree. As a result, after two and a half years of completed studies, a double degree student can receive two degrees: a U.S. MBA and a Finnish Master of Science in Economics and Business Administration.

## Background of the Double Degree Cooperation

The program dates back to fall 2004, when the rector of the University of Oulu awarded the Oulu Business School a grant to further develop its international cooperation toward a double degree program. In consideration of possible cooperation partners, the UNCG was seen as a preferable partner on the basis of two specific issues. First, since 1993 the universities had actively exchanged students, during which time trusting relationships had been developed, especially between the personnel of the International Study Offices. Second, the UNCG has a high-quality, accredited MBA program that was expected to be both beneficial and interesting to Finnish business students. In June 2005, the associate director of the MBA program of the Bryan School of Business visited the University of Oulu to meet the personnel and have discussions about the possibilities for double degree cooperation. In January 2006, after active email correspondence between the schools, the delegation of the rector of the University of Oulu visited Greensboro. Together with the president of the UNCG and the deans of both business schools, he signed the actual agreement on double degree cooperation. The first students aiming to complete the double degree were selected at the Oulu Business School in spring 2006, and they started their studies at the Bryan School of Business in fall 2006.

## Student Selection for the Double Degree Studies

As business studies and degrees in Finland and the U.S. have significant differences, selecting students who are likely to be able to complete both degrees is not a simple process. The first major challenge is that a typical Finnish bachelor's degree is focused on one major subject, whereas a typical U.S. bachelor's degree in business contains the basics of all main business subjects (such as accounting, economics, finance, management, and marketing) as well as several mathematics and statistics courses. In addition, the Finnish students tend to have significant freedom in their choice of minor subjects and the order of course completion during the bachelor's degree. As the U.S. MBA is also a general management degree consisting of studies in all major business subjects, the students selected for the MBA program need to have wide basic knowledge, which is checked through a list of necessary background studies in the agreement between the universities. Since the Oulu Business School students are able to receive their bachelor's degree without having completed the basics of all the main business subjects, they may need to study one or two extra basic courses in order to study at the UNCG as a degree-seeking student. This can be seen as the first test of motivation for the Finnish students.

In addition to these necessary background studies, the Finnish students need to have a certain amount of other background studies that allow them to waive some basic MBA courses and make it possible to complete the required MBA studies in one academic year. This means that the business schools have developed another list of courses that can be substituted one for the other. From the viewpoint of the student selection process, this means that student transcripts and credits are also evaluated. Some students' individual study backgrounds may not be suitable for double degree studies in the anticipated timeframe. Or they may need to complete one or two extra courses again in Oulu.

The third challenge is that the Oulu Business School students have to complete the same tests as the other foreign students who come to study in the MBA program of the UNCG as degree-seeking students. In practice, this means TOEFL and GMAT tests with defined test scores. In Finland, the tests are administered only in Helsinki and only on certain dates. The students may need to practice for the tests in addition to finding time to travel to Helsinki on some of the available dates. Students need to do a lot of organizing to fit practice and test taking in between their courses in Finland. Again, this is quite a test for the student's motivation and organizing skills.

Fourth, the applicants need to exhibit high academic achievement in their bachelor's degree studies to be accepted to the UNCG as MBA degree-seeking students. A student who has been very motivated from the beginning and has been aware of the specific requirements for double degree studies will be able to fulfill these selection criteria through a smooth process. This kind of student can plan to complete the background studies for the three years of bachelor's studies, perform at a high academic level, and plan for the tests in good time without stress. However, it is quite typical for a student to become interested in this kind of special opportunity quite unexpectedly and without a long-term plan. This easily means that the final year of the bachelor's degree studies is a very busy and potentially stressful one for a student who has just decided to pursue selection as a double degree-seeking student.

Our tasks in the Oulu Business School focus on making sure that the students we suggest as applicants to the double degree studies at the UNCG fulfill these background requirements. At this stage, in mid-April, we send the whole application and the student transcripts to the associate director of the MBA program at the UNCG. Her office personnel will now verify that the students can be accepted and are able to complete the required MBA studies during the next academic year. The study program is tailored to each student on the basis of the student's background studies. The chosen students study as normal exchange students their first semester in the UNCG. During the first semester, the students still have to fulfill the requirement of achieving the minimum GPA of 3.0, and only then may they apply to become degree-seeking students in the Bryan School of Business. As degree-seeking students, they also need to pay tuition and course fees for the spring semester. Only then is the selection process completed from the student's point of view.

## Overcoming the Challenges

Due to the short history of the double degree cooperation between the Oulu Business School and the Bryan School of Business, the student selection process has been further developed every year. Gradually, we achieve a process that is smooth both from the students' and the universities' point of view. To support the selection process, we currently have agreed-on lists of necessary background courses from the Oulu Business School and substitute courses that allow waiving some basic courses of the MBA degree. One of the key elements in successful double degree cooperation is the credit transfer system that has been created. When the schools apply studies from each other's curricula to the degree, it is important to agree in advance on criteria concerning the level of courses and required grades. In our case, the representatives of the business schools stated in an early phase of cooperation that crediting of the MBA and master's-level courses can be done bilaterally. As contents and methods of teaching naturally differ between schools and courses, the main idea was to concentrate on the higher level of the courses (master's) instead of the exact content. The established criteria also help students to evaluate their own situation as an applicant.

The solutions created in this cooperation are developed primarily from the students' point of view. For example, after three years' experience, the crediting of courses has been developed notably thanks to student feedback and close cooperation between the schools. The process has taken some time, but as a result students now have a clear vision of their degrees. In creating these degree contents, many emails, including course descriptions, were sent, and several professors were asked to evaluate the similarities between the two schools' courses. This matchmaking has probably been the most demanding part of the double degree cooperation so far.

If counted from the very beginning, each selection process takes us over one year. We inform students of the possibility of double degree studies in cooperation with the International Study Office's information days for normal exchange studies during the spring semesters. At the beginning of the fall semesters we organize a business school briefing about double degree studies. These two occasions are meant to allow students to learn about the possibility and start to prepare for it as early as possible. We also have a multistep selection process scheduled for students at the Oulu Business School. An important part of the selection process consists of personal interaction with the interested students and possible applicants on the basis of their individual study backgrounds and planned studies. Often this interaction covers the whole academic year prior to their planned studies in the UNCG.

Each year we have noted a growing interest in the double degree program among Oulu Business School students. Several students have also achieved or are just about to achieve double degrees through this program. The students see the program as a once in a lifetime opportunity to receive two recognized degrees that give an advantage in today's working life.

## Transatlantic Degree Program – At a Glance

| | |
|---|---|
| Name of Program | International Double Degree Program |
| Partner Institutions | Oulu Business School of the University of Oulu, Finland<br><br>Bryan School of Business and Economics of the University of North Carolina at Greensboro, U.S. |
| Location of Study | Oulu, Finland and Greensboro, U.S. |
| Academic Field(s) | Economics and Business Administration |
| Academic Level | Master |

| Year Started | 2006 | What type of degree is awarded? | Double |
|---|---|---|---|

| Language(s) of Instruction | Finnish and English |
|---|---|

How many students participated in the most recent year of the program?

| | EU students | 2 | U.S. students | 0 | Other students | |
|---|---|---|---|---|---|---|

How many students have graduated from the program since it began?

| | EU students | 4 | U.S. students | 0 | Other students | |
|---|---|---|---|---|---|---|

# FACILITATING JOINT DEGREES THROUGH JOINT OWNERSHIP

BY KATHLEEN E. MURPHY AND PAUL TOMKINS

Inter-institutional collaboration for purposes of teaching and research has become a major action for most higher education institutions in developed countries, and cross-border collaboration that drives the internationalization of education is continuously growing in scale and significance (Knight, 2008). In the past, most inter-institutional agreements were well-suited to short-term exchanges and development of "casual" relationships between the partner institutions. However, a trend is emerging for the development of more meaningful relationships in which each partner can benefit in ways other than a simple student exchange (Fischer, 2009). Although potentially much more sustainable and mutually beneficial to the institutions involved, these new types of agreements by their nature are more selective and require a level of planning and framework not employed in the more "casual" framework. The awarding of a trans-atlantic joint degree falls into the latter category. Because joint degree programs strive to become part of each institution's structure, they must do more than add to the list of courses offered at each institution. Consequently, most of these collaborations must include an avenue for faculty research, coupled with student participation, to become sustainable and valuable to the partner institutions.

From the perspective of developing and delivering a joint degree with inter-national partners, a number of factors must be considered as critical in the planning and implementation phases. Of these, an important first step in establishing a dynamic, sustainable collaboration is to include several facets of effective communi-cation. As with any collaborative project, there are a number of basic and core attrib-utes that can contribute to the sustainable success of the interaction:

- All parties are aware of the mutual and complementary benefits that collabo-ration brings.

- At least two key individual partner members have a history of good personal rela-tions to serve as the permanent basis of knowledge and trust for the partnership.

- All partners are aware of and understand the operational structures of each respective institution on a departmental as well as institutional level, including such matters as the academic calendar, student health records, student accommodation requirements, and quality control/assessment models.

- Regular communication and interaction between partner faculty contributes to effective communication and development of mutual trust.

- Faculty exchanges and/or partner site visits are a critical component to allow partners to determine how their students will "fit" into the other institution's structure and to potentially evaluate the difference(s) in course content and teaching structures.

- A mutually discussed and agreed-upon project plan, albeit an evolving one, needs to be adopted. Adjustments to the plan and measures of compliance should be a subject of annual meetings.

- Academic and management communication networks need to be established.

- Communications technology, where viable (video conferencing), needs to be applied.

- Records of all formal meetings must be retained and all feedback responded to.

- Respective student experiences need to be sufficiently positive to feedback and to enforce partner communication and collaboration.

- At least one high-level administrator such as college or university president, chancellor or provost, who can act as a "champion" for the collaboration at each lead partner institution, needs to "buy in."

Since the early 1980s, inter-institutional collaboration has been a core feature of EU research, and the Erasmus program has embedded a culture of inter-institutional student mobility. Models of cooperation can be extended to transatlantic degrees and serve as the basis for a continuing relationship. Bilateral agreements can more easily be built between institutions as a network united by a common research agenda organized around a broad theme, which allows for greater participation of diverse faculty at the partner institutions.

Higher education (HE) collaborations can be established following a strategic analysis of what would be valuable and complementary partners, but typically the founding seed for collaborations is some degree of prior personal relationship. Personal relationships also incentivize some partners to join a partnership (Amey et al., 2007). Sociability and interpersonal skills directly relate to norms of collegiality and collaboration. Not surprisingly, employers have identified these two elements as desirable traits for the workplace (Uchiyama & Radin, 2009). Strong partnerships are a basis for developing a common understanding of goals and assessment standards. Personal relationships allow a flexible and much deeper understanding to develop, and partners can then better assess whether they have similar expectations for their students.

Collaboration implies interdependency and joint ownership of decisions and inherently involves the development of a project plan that identifies issues and targets, milestones, and implementation goals. Curriculum development and pedagogies can be a basis for collaboration between higher education institutions (HEIs) (Sa et al., 2003); Donahue, 2008; Uchiyama & Radin, 2009). As we have already suggested, for collaboration to be sustained there must be perceived benefits for all the parties involved (Connolly et al., 2007). Reflection on program delivery as a basis for understanding what has and has not worked is accepted as good practice (Bernacchio et al., 2007).

A recent report from the Observatory on Borderless Education emphasizes the role of day-to-day endeavors and staff links in forging strong institutional bonds, in the belief that for sustainable alliances, it is the recurrent input and activity of academics that matters most (Gore, 2008). The importance of academic networks to support collaboration is a recognized benefit (Marino, 2002). The key role played by well-connected faculty in initiating and driving alliances implies that HEIs must know about and encourage international networking by staff (Marino, 2002). The report also advises that having the right people involved is crucial to program success, which demands strategic, "top-down" management of the "bottom-up" networking process. Trust can be achieved through prolonged contact and shared activity. Contacts and memoranda of agreement formalize relationships but are obviously inadequate without the underlying people engagements.

There are numerous examples of international collaborative degree programs (Burnard, 1994; Sa et al., 2003; Ayoubi et al., 2006; Smith et al., 2006; Griffiths, 2003; Spellerberg et al., 2007). The key "people" engagements must be between the faculty at the partner institutions. Successful partnerships outlast the time many administrators spend in a single position, so it is very important that the key parts of the project be grounded in the faculty segment of the institution.

In terms of an optimal partner structure that supports collaboration and effective communication, we would recommend the model depicted in Figure 1. As previously indicated, engagement of the right people, commitment, a project plan, and good personal relationships are all important elements of a successful collaborative HE project, and all such partnerships normally work on the basis of inter-institutional agreements. To focus on this action and generate a critical mass of engaged academics and additional resources, we propose the establishment of a formal jointly owned entity. This could be a nonprofit organization or a center or institute in which each partner HEI has an equal share. While this is predominantly a virtual structure, the participating staff in each partner institution are effectively assigned to the entity, with the lead European and U.S. partners representing a management structure for the organization. This model could be employed to deliver HEI-HEI and HEI-industry partnerships to deliver collaborative research as well as joint degrees, and indeed such an entity can participate in multiple outcomes. A percentage of the budget or preferably a contribution on behalf of each partner is employed to fund administration and web services. Creation of such an academic vehicle automatically generates a series of benefits:

- In delivering a program, the number of participating faculty or staff engaged in specialist modules in each institution is likely to be relatively small. The collective group across all partners, as represented by the joint entity, becomes significant, and the entity provides a forum for course review, development, and other academic interactions.

- The existence of a joint entity delivering the program provides a very visible focus for all staff and students and provides a forum for the sharing of information between partners.

- The joint entity will support video conference communication between the relevant staff at each partner HEI.

- With a unique composition of academics across institutions but in a common discipline, with a management and administration structure, the entity will inevitably develop a sustainability plan and attract additional sources of revenue.

- The joint entity provides a vehicle for other collaborative projects—research, international education policy development, and communication with the wider community in each partner country.

- If the educational delivery by the consortium involves industry partners for placement or specialist module delivery, the joint entity can provide a more efficient and business-compatible interface.

- The joint entity provides a driver and mechanism for joint publications.

A collaborative entity model has become a significant basis for research growth in Scotland. The Scottish Universities Physics Alliance (SUPA), the Scottish University Life Sciences Alliance (SULSA), and HealthQWest, for example, are significant research alliances in physics, biology, and nonmedical healthcare across a number of universities. Researcher membership in such an entity creates a working environment that extends beyond loyalty to the employer institution. Staff members innately feel part of a larger organization, which projects its own strategy, mission, and functioning criteria. The benefits of creating such a center and consequential relationships will positively impact each partner institution department, mediating knowledge transfer and the generation of additional collaboration projects.

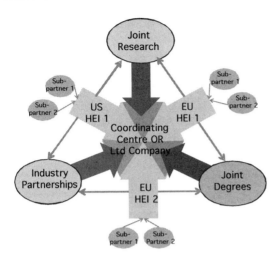

Note: The figure is a generic depiction and includes two EU and one U.S. HEI, according to the basic structure of EU-U.S. Atlantis Program joint degrees. Actual coordinating centers might accommodate different numbers of partner institutions. All HEIs linked to the center are engaged in joint degree development and delivery. Outside arrows represent potential links to collaborative research, interaction with industry, and other partnership projects.

REFERENCES

Amey, M.J., Eddy, P.L., & Ozaki, C.C. (2007). Demands for partnership and collaboration in higher education: A model. *New Directions for Community Colleges,* 5-14.

Ayoubi, R.M., & Al-Habaibeh, A. (2006). An investigation into international business collaboration in higher education organizations: A case study of international partnerships in four UK leading universities. *International Journal of Educational Management, 20,* 380-396.

Bernacchio, C., Ross, F., Washburn, K. R., Whitney, J., & Wood, D. R. (2007). Faculty collaboration to improve equity, access, and inclusion in higher education. *Equity and Excellence in Education, 40,* 56-66.

Burnard, P. (1994). Planning international nursing courses: A new degree course that aims to reflect the increasingly international nature of nursing. *Nursing Standard – London, 8,* 24.

Connolly, M., Jones, C., & Jones, N. (2007). Managing collaboration across further and higher education: A case in practice. *Journal of Further and Higher Education* 3, 159-169.

Fischer, K. (2009). US colleges get serious with partners overseas. *Chronicle of Higher Education,* 55, A21.

Gore, T. (2008). Global research collaboration: The UKIERI India-UK initiative – Lessons from practice for sustainable international partnerships. The Observatory on Borderless Higher Education.

Griffiths, M. (2003). Policy-practice proximity: The scope for college-based higher education and cross-sector collaboration in Wales. *Higher Education Quarterly, 57,* 355-375.

Knight, J. (2008). Higher education in turmoil: The changing world of internationalisation. Rotterdam: Sense Publishers.

Marino, S. (2002). Creating networks through inter-institutional faculty collaboration. *New Directions for Higher Education*: 55-62.

Sa, E., Sekikawa, A., Linkov, F., Lovalekar, M., & LaPorte, R. E. (2003). Open source model for global collaboration in higher education. *International Journal of Medical Informatics, 71*, 165.

Smith, R., Terry, A., & Vibhakar, A. (2006). Increasingly global: Combining an international business degree with a post-degree designation. *Journal of Teaching in International Business, 18*, 53-72.

Spellerberg, I. F., Loiskandl, W, & Buchan, G. (2007). A joint, international masters degree in sustainability: How a truly global programme was established. *International Journal of Environment and Sustainable Development, 6*, 67-80.

Uchiyama, K.P., & Radin, J.L. (2009). Curriculum mapping in higher education: A vehicle for collaboration. *Innovative Higher Education - New York, 33*, 271-280.

# Transatlantic Degree Program – At a Glance

| | | | | |
|---|---|---|---|---|
| Name of Program | Biotechnology in Healthcare | | | |
| Partner Institutions | Daemen College<br>Pitzer College<br>New College<br>University of Birkenfelt<br>University of Kokola<br>Athlone Institute of Technology | | | |
| Location of Study | All partner sites | | | |
| Academic Field(s) | Biotechnology, toxicology, chemistry, healthcare | | | |
| Academic Level | BSc | | | |
| Year Started | 2005 | What type of degree is awarded? | See note | |
| Language(s) of Instruction | | English | | |
| How many students participated in the most recent year of the program? | | | | |
| | EU students | 4 | U.S. students | 5 | Other students | 0 |
| How many students have completed the program since it began? | | | | |
| | EU students | 23 | U.S. students | 18 | Other students | 3 |

Note: the BIHC programme represents a precursor to a full joint degree. Students transferred for one semester and were awarded appropriate credits. The consortium will seek to launch a full joint degree employing the coordinating center model.

# Interpersonal Relationships and the Sustainability of Cooperative Degree Programs

By Jeffrey W. Steagall, Jeffrey Michelman, and Anne Sheridan Fugard

Creating a new cooperative degree program is fraught with challenges. In many cases, the energy expended by the program organizers and the political capital that they expend to solve implementation issues at their home universities can lead them to have a rather laissez-faire approach to the program once it begins. Such an approach is erroneous. Cooperative degree programs require continuous oversight and hands-on management to a far greater degree than do traditional, on-campus programs.

This article examines the effect that the departure of a key individual at one partner institution can have on the viability of any cooperative degree program. Two principles underlie the recommendations. First, there must be strong interpersonal relationships among the program leaders at consortium partners. Second, faculty members' interests evolve over time. Faculty might change duties or even move to a new university, requiring their resignation from program leadership. Therefore, such interpersonal relationships must be robust, extending beyond a single person to potential new leadership candidates when a leadership transition occurs. *Personal* relationships drive programs, but *institutional* relationships must sustain them.

The recommendations here result from an issue that arose in a double-degree program in which the authors' university participates. The GlobalMBA program (http://GlobalMBA.unf.edu) is a 15-month double master's degree program now offered by a consortium of four universities, including the Cologne University of Applied Sciences (CUAS), Germany; the University of Warsaw (UW), Poland; Dongbei University of Finance and Economics (DUFE), China; and the University of North Florida (UNF). Each university selects 10 students to participate in the 40-student cohort that begins every October. The cohort studies together for one semester at each university, with all instruction in English. Graduation results in two degrees—an MBA from UNF and a joint Master of International Management and Intercultural Communication from CUAS and UW—as well as a certificate of participation from DUFE, for each student. Interested readers are referred to Steagall, Michelman, and Traynham (2004) for a blueprint of how to set up a cooperative degree program based on the GlobalMBA experience.

Cooperative degree programs require a significant commitment not only from the universities involved, but also, and much more critically, from the individual program leaders at each institution. Indeed, cooperative degree programs often depend critically on the relationships among the program directors, whose commitments to one another are typically stronger than the inter-institutional commitments.

This reality struck the GlobalMBA program during the summer of 2006, when the program director at one original partner institution was promoted from his department-head position to a vice-presidential office. With extensive new duties, he was unable to continue to lead the GlobalMBA at his institution. Unfortunately, no other faculty member in the department was willing to replace him, leaving that institution no option but to withdraw from the consortium. This withdrawal presented three major challenges for the remaining institutions: students planning to participate in the program now had nowhere to go for its second semester, a leadership transition plan needed to be developed at each university, and a new replacement partner had to be identified and courted.

With respect to the first challenge, due to the timing of the promotion, the withdrawal occurred within six weeks of the beginning of a new cohort program. Obviously, all institutions had already selected students for the program, and students had made plans to participate. Although the consortium agreement required one year's notice of withdrawal, it was clear that there was no realistic possibility to operate the program without the departing faculty member's leadership. Attempting to enforce this condition seemed to be in nobody's best interests. The partners determined that the only viable course of action was to put the program on hiatus for one year, during which they would seek and integrate a new partner.

The second challenge involved formal transition planning. To ensure smooth leadership transitions, cooperative degree programs must have institutional support rather than depend wholly on a single faculty member occupying a specific position. Indeed, the consortium members were aware that support for the GlobalMBA from the department at that university was weak. Moreover, despite multiple meetings of the consortium's program directors at that university, no additional personal relationships were developed—the program and even contact with the university depended entirely on a single individual. The failure of the program directors to ensure that a transition plan existed resulted in a year's cancellation of the program and the disruption of the plans for a large group of students.

The key question, of course, is how to ensure an institutional commitment. Three solutions seem plausible, and all focus on the faculty who teach in the program, since they often develop an affinity for the program and its students. The program leader on each campus should ensure that the other program leaders meet and spend time getting to know the faculty members teaching in the program. It is further recommended that such interactions not be limited to an official meeting in a university conference room. Extended social time, such as a consortium-sponsored dinner, will allow the diverse group to relax and become acquainted more profoundly than they could in a formal setting. The value of the interpersonal connections will greatly exceed the cost of the dinner. If the program leader moves on, there is a pool of individuals with a vested interest in sustaining the program, even if one of them must assume its leadership.

A second solution is to deepen faculty connections using research as the vehicle. The GlobalMBA partners now co-sponsor research seminars, and faculty members from all four institutions participate routinely. They not only interact in the scholarly arena but also get to know one another personally at conference meals, breaks, etc. Moreover, joint research projects across institutions have developed naturally. The consortium is therefore much better prepared to survive the departure of a program leader than in the past.

The third solution, of course, is that each institution and each program leader must always be grooming a replacement for the existing director. That can happen most effectively through the formal designation of an assistant program director (although such appointments often generate expenses for the university, often in the form of a slightly reduced teaching load) but may also occur less formally through mentorship by the current program leader.

The third challenge for the program directors was to replace the exiting partner. Discussions began immediately, with the directors identifying key desirable characteristics based on lessons they had learned from developing and sustaining the GlobalMBA. Some requirements were obvious. The new partner needed full accreditation and the ability to deliver the appropriate courses in English. Moreover, because the existing schools had all accredited the program, the new partner would have very little input into the courses that it would offer. The new institution would have to be willing to agree to such a limitation and have the expertise to teach the necessary courses. It needed to be willing to identify a student-services person who would be in charge of the GlobalMBA students to help them with matriculation, lodging, etc., since it had been determined through student feedback that such an individual in each location was essential.

The existing partners also had a strong preference to identify an institution that had an active, smoothly operating relationship with one of the remaining partners. In addition to eliminating the need to develop new inter-institutional relationships, using an existing partner would ensure that the personal relationships that are so important for program success would already be at an advanced stage. Fortunately, since the GlobalMBA enjoyed a strong reputation at each university, many existing partners already knew about it and had expressed interest in joining it at some point. In fact, the University of Warsaw joined the original three-university consortium in 2005 through its strong ties to the University of North Florida. After discussing several possible partners, the consortium agreed to approach DUFE, a partner of CUAS. While DUFE's quality and the very strong ties at the vice-presidential level were points in its favor, the consortium also had a strong preference to add a Chinese partner to provide students with more diversity in the program.

Despite the strong existing CUAS-DUFE linkages, many details had to be negotiated in order for DUFE to join the consortium. One of these, of course, was to determine whether DUFE wanted to join. The program directors therefore visited DUFE in October 2006 for two intensive days of meetings, during which it was clear that DUFE and the GlobalMBA were well-matched from everyone's perspective. Thus, DUFE joined the consortium for the 2007/08 cohort, both sending students through the program and delivering a semester of courses. The strong institutional relationships between CUAS and DUFE have now expanded to include strong personal relationships between DUFE's faculty, staff, and program director and their counterparts at CUAS, UW, and UNF.

In summary, interpersonal relationships remain the foundation of any cooperative degree program. Without them, the programs are unsustainable. However, one danger of strong relationships is the fallacy that they can last forever. Careers evolve, and program leaders may opt to explore new opportunities. Partners must plan for such eventualities, not only through statements in the consortium agreements but also by developing solid transition plans at every university. Moreover, directors must immediately begin to develop personal relationships with the next-generation program leaders, so that when the transition occurs, there is no gap in program coherence or continuance. The goal is to ensure that relationships extend beyond single individuals to become institutional in nature, with multiple faculty and staff connecting across any pair of partners.

*The authors thank their GlobalMBA colleagues, Lothar Černy, Harald Sander, Dagmar Schall, Alojzy Nowak, David Wang, and Tracy Liu for their proactive, solution-oriented work developing and operating the GlobalMBA program. They have provided the inspiration for this article's suggestions.*

REFERENCES

Steagall, J.W., Michaelman, J.E., & Traynham, E.C. (2004). GlobalMBA: A blueprint for creating an integrated, international trilateral MBA program. *Journal of Teaching in International Business, 16/1*, 7-23.

# Transatlantic Degree Program – At a Glance

| | | | | | |
|---|---|---|---|---|---|
| Name of Program | GlobalMBA | | | | |
| Partner Institutions | Cologne University of Applied Sciences (Germany) University of Warsaw (Poland) Dongbei University of Finance & Economics (China) University of North Florida (U.S.) | | | | |
| Location of Study | Cologne, Germany; Warsaw, Poland; Dalian, China; and Jacksonville, Florida (U.S.) | | | | |
| Academic Field(s) | Intercultural Communications & Business Administration | | | | |
| Academic Level | Graduate | | | | |
| Year Started | 2001 | What type of degree is awarded? | Double | | |
| Language(s) of Instruction | | English | | | |
| How many students participated in the most recent year of the program? | | | | | |
| | EU students | 14 | U.S. students | 9 | Other students | 0 |
| How many students have graduated from the program since it began? | | | | | |
| | EU students | 63 | U.S. students | 35 | Other students | 3 |

# Beyond Funding: Sustainability and the TransAtlantic Masters (TAM) Program

By Sarah A. Hutchison

Discussions of joint and double degree programs often point to important challenges in securing institutional support and funding. Though money matters remain an unquestionably crucial concern as many of us seek to grow international and inter-institutional programs, efforts to ensure a program's sustainability must have a broader reach. Many equate a program's financial viability with its means to endure; however, the cultivation of a strong alumni network from day one will also yield a valuable resource to help the program continue. Graduates can play a major role in a program's long-term success. Ultimately, expanding the concept of sustainability to include alumni development will come full circle and again focus on money when graduates are in a position to make financial contributions to the program. Yet other forms of alumni giving such as internships, professional information, or site visits can be significantly more substantive, meaningful, and valuable than a personal check.

The following article underscores the reasons joint and double degree programs in particular need to foster the program cohesion an alumni network can offer, and also details some of the successful alumni-development strategies in place within the TransAtlantic Masters (TAM) Program at the University of North Carolina at Chapel Hill (UNC-CH). The TAM Program may not fit the classic definition of a joint or double degree, since TAM students receive a single degree from one institution. But the idea of fostering sustainability through alumni networks is one that administrators of joint and dual degree programs should consider as their programs grow over the coming years.

One of the most important defining features of a transatlantic joint or dual degree program is the opportunity for students to study on two or more campuses and across national boundaries. This experience enables students to join multiple communities. For most, this is an exciting prospect—to benefit from the resources of more than one institution of higher learning, to experience more than one culture, and potentially to put one's foreign language skills to use. While these opportunities are valuable and sought-after by many an applicant, the very nature of joint and double degree programs may leave a participant feeling disconnected from a home base.

This disjointed status may inevitably make it more difficult for students to connect with one or more specific institutions, and to stay connected after they have graduated. Participants in the TAM Program, for instance, spend up to three-quarters of their time studying at one or more of our partner sites in Europe. Partner sites include the University of Bath in England, SciencesPo in Paris, Carlos III University in Madrid, Charles University in Prague, VU University in Amsterdam, Universitat Pompeu Fabra in Barcelona, University of Siena in Italy, Humboldt University in Berlin, and Freie Universität Berlin. The students are thus distanced from TAM's base at UNC-CH for significant periods of time. In order to bridge this physical space, the program can and should create opportunities for applicants, students, and alumni to feel connected to one another and to assume a shared programmatic identity.

In more than six years as TAM's student services director, and in my more recent role as the program's associate director, I have been pleased to see our administrators and faculty members take an active interest in each TAM student as an individual and in each cohort as a distinctive group. We enjoy certain luxuries—our largest incoming class ever consisted of 27 students—that make one-on-one interaction possible. In addition, our student body is comprised of diverse young people who enter the program with well-formed academic and professional goals. In short, it is a pleasure and a privilege to get to know them. Faculty members have the chance to learn about their students during class time as well as during TAM-sponsored social events. Many of our visiting scholars and lecturers have gone out of their way to invite TAM students they have met in Chapel Hill out to meals, lectures, or even sporting events once the students arrive in Europe. These spontaneous efforts show the students that they are a valued part of our TAM network.

As an administrator, I have the chance to communicate and interact with TAM applicants, students, and alumni. The most rewarding part of my job involves following the trajectory of these individuals as they make their way through the program and into their careers. I have frequent contact with the students, but the most meaningful interactions are my one-on-one meetings with them at the start of the program to discuss internship opportunities as well as the less formal chances I have to speak with them during our fall break trip to Washington, D.C. As I get to know the students on a more personal basis, I become better equipped to help them achieve their academic and professional goals. For the most part I accomplish this by putting students in touch with TAM graduates with whom they share interests.

During our annual student trip to D.C., which typically involves site visits and briefings at institutions such as the World Bank, the Pentagon, the Delegation of the European Commission, and the U.S. Department of State, we organize a party and invite all graduates of the program to attend and meet the current students. Our highest concentration of alumni can be found in D.C., and typically 30-40 graduates attend—a significant number given that the entire alumni population totals less than 200. Before the trip, I distribute brief student and alumni bios to the alumni and students, respectively. Students are, of course, eager to glimpse the professional opportunities that await them. The graduates are no less eager to meet the individuals who now fill their shoes in the program. This annual gathering provides graduates with an opportunity to stay connected to TAM and to learn of the program's developments. We also hold a smaller current student-alumni event in Europe each spring.

In response to alumni feedback, during the fall orientation session and during our pre-D.C. departure meeting, I tell students what they can and cannot expect from their interaction with a TAM graduate. "No one is going to hand you a job on a silver platter," I explain. The alumni are, however, happy to share their experiences and to answer specific questions. In the past, some graduates have let me know that they have felt badgered or under-valued by students. I welcome this alumni feedback and provide anecdotal evidence (all names are changed) to students to illustrate what is and is not acceptable behavior. My purpose here is two-fold: (1) Students receive specific instructions such as: When you receive an email response from a graduate, you need to answer that email and thank the alumnus or alumna. Forewarned students are thus less likely to irritate a TAM graduate. Though I would like to believe that this kind of tutorial in basic manners is unnecessary for most, experience has shown that many of our students do need refresher courses in etiquette. (2) As expectations are made clear, students start to get an early sense of how they will eventually give back to the program and to future students once they graduate.

Over the years, graduates who have stayed engaged with the program have contributed to its success in many ways. Their continued interest in the program's growth inspires confidence among students. TAM graduates have volunteered to communicate with prospective students. They have hosted student groups in their workplaces during the D.C. trip. They have shared their employment experiences with recent graduates. They have let me know about job opportunities where they work so that I can publicize them to other graduates. In some cases, alumni have even directly helped fellow TAM graduates secure jobs. They have contributed money to our Friends of TAM Account, which is designed to provide tuition remissions to international students. As the program has grown, we have appointed class officers to collect news updates from classmates for our annual alumni newsletter, we have conferred a distinguished alumna award, and we have maintained a confidential database with information about TAM employment histories. Newer initiatives involve the use of online social networking tools such as Facebook and LinkedIn to foster a sense of community among far-flung TAM populations.

Program graduates are an invaluable resource and play a direct role in program sustainability. When program administrators and faculty members offer students and alumni opportunities to voice opinions and make suggestions, an atmosphere of collaboration and co-ownership will result. As one strategizes for the critical financial viability of a joint or dual degree program, it is important to cultivate a sense of program cohesion and identity. These efforts will foster meaningful and continued involvement on the part of students and alumni and will ultimately make it possible for the program to thrive.

# Transatlantic Degree Program – At a Glance

| Name of Program | TransAtlantic Masters Program | | | | |
|---|---|---|---|---|---|
| Partner Institutions | University of North Carolina at Chapel Hill (UNC-CH) <br> Humboldt University (Berlin) <br> Freie Universität Berlin, Sciences-Po (Paris) <br> Carlos III University (Madrid) <br> University of Siena <br> VU University Amsterdam <br> Universitat Pompeu Fabra (Barcelona) <br> Bath University <br> Charles University (Prague) | | | | |
| Location of Study | U.S. and Europe | | | | |
| Academic Field(s) | Political Science | | | | |
| Academic Level | Master's | | | | |
| Year Started | 1998 | What type of degree is awarded? | | Single Degrees | |
| Language(s) of Instruction | | English, Spanish, French, German and Italian | | | |
| How many students participated in the most recent year of the program? | | | | | |
| | EU students | 10 | U.S. students | 17 | Other students | 0 |
| How many students have graduated from the program since it began? | | | | | |
| | EU students | 20 | U.S. students | 146 | Other students | 8 |

# TREE: An International Four-Year Dual Degree Program for Students of Economics

By El Nault

The TransAtlantic Exchange in Economics (TREE) project is a four-year dual degree program jointly funded by the U.S. Department of Education's Fund for the Improvement of Postsecondary Education (FIPSE) and the European Commission's Directorate General for Education and Culture. The TREE Atlantis program contributes to EU-U.S. international academic cooperation through offering students both a BA in economics from Clemson University and a baccalaureate in sciences economiques et gestion from Université Catholique de Louvain (UCL).

Clemson is public, southern research institution and one of 300 international universities with which UCL has a signed agreement. Because of the complexity of the agreement between Clemson and UCL, several design issues were identified and reconciled during early stages of the program. The EU requirement that participating students attend two EU institutions required the engagement of a third university. The Universiteit Maastricht (UM) was selected because the faculty of UCL and UM have worked together under other agreements. UCL and Clemson had been engaged in a student exchange program and were familiar with many of the academic expectations. However, faculty and student exchanges are quite simple compared to highly competitive, approved academic degree programs. Without the foundation of the exchange program that supports the notion that good working relations between institutions are necessary to assure any successful project, the dual degree programs would have not begun as early in the EU-U.S. joint grant approval processes.

Meeting degree requirements is grounded in understanding the expectations of the university, academic department, and other governing entities. At Clemson, all degree programs or significant modifications to programs are established by the faculty with approval by the board of trustees, the state higher education commission, and the regional accreditation commission. The TREE project built upon an existing degree program and therefore was exempt from the necessary processes to establish a new program. This did not alleviate the many difficulties that arise when integrating two different programs and cultures into one project. Two primary problems were the recruitment of students into cohorts and establishing course and degree requirements. Specific challenges and solutions to each of these are discussed in the following sections.

## Cohort Design and Recruitment

Background: Intentional Design

A cohort design was selected for the TREE program because it provides students from both universities with an opportunity to attend classes and live in communities with each other for over two years. At Clemson, the students must be identified and committed to the program early in their university experience, since sufficient time must be left for the students to return after attending the EU universities to complete their required 37 hours on campus. The Clemson students attend two European universities as a part of the program, attending UM during the second semester of the sophomore year and UCL for the entire junior year. Clemson students then return to Clemson their senior year. The cohort of UCL students attend UM, UCL, and Clemson at the same time as the Clemson students in their cohort. Thus, the Clemson students spend one year and the first semester of the second year at their home institution with the cohort activities commencing the second semester of the second year. After completing the course work in the EU, the students graduate from UCL. They then continue with their coursework at Clemson and graduate as a cohort in the fourth year.

Participation Criteria

The program is open to all students at Clemson. However, there are specific criteria that each student must meet prior to entry into the program: 1) the student must be fluent in French in order to take challenging upper division business courses in French, 2) the student must complete the foundation courses in economics and math in order to succeed in the rigorous UCL and UM courses, and 3) the student must meet the financial obligations associated with enrollment and exchange programs. The UCL program is an economics and management program, so the Clemson students must complete six business courses (the equivalent of a minor in business) prior to attending UCL. It is difficult to recruit freshmen students who meet all of these expectations; few students who enroll in economics or language and international trade have the necessary French literacy and math skills by the beginning of their second semester second year. Thus, the pool of applicants into the dual degree program and cohort participation is highly restricted. Typically, students who enter the university with advanced placement credits in French or who study French for two or three semesters possess a conversational level of French. If students must take French courses, these are most frequently taken in addition to the regular load of required program courses and the pre-departure courses required for the business minor.

## Semester Offerings

The importance of coordinated exchanges is based on the fact that the classes needed for the programs are not offered every semester. To ensure progress toward meeting the degree requirements, coordinating student enrollment in correct class sequence continues to benefit the advisors and students in knowing when to expect the transfer students and the specific courses that are required.

## Curriculum Requirements

### Background: Degree Program Design

As is the case at UCL, the degree program curriculum at CU is developed and maintained by the departmental faculty. However, unlike UCL, Clemson has governing bodies and accreditation agencies that have adopted specific criteria that must be addressed by or incorporated into the curriculum, including the mandate for a general education experience. The learning outcomes associated with general education are typically obtained by taking classes outside of the discipline. In addition to the traditional general education courses, Clemson has general education outcomes that are delivered within the discipline content.

### Credit Hours and Courses

An institutional hurdle to be overcome was the traditional acceptance of the European Credit Transfer and Accumulation System (ECTS). The ECTS is one of the key elements of the Bologna Declaration of 1999, signed by 45 countries, intending to develop a comparable educational system across national boundaries. It was developed to be a student-centered system of giving credit to coursework based on the number of student learning hours needed to accomplish the intended educational outcomes of a certain course or of an entire program. After intensive conversations, it was noted that the ECTS would be useful if the faculty were not familiar with the courses, content, or other aspects of integrated programs. The Clemson and UCL faculty agreed upon the transfer of courses and expectations of courses to be taken at the partners' schools. This was accomplished through the face-to-face discussions and classroom observations. Additionally, the syllabi were reviewed, content was discussed, textbooks were examined, and other intense collaborative efforts were made by the faculty to ensure that each of the courses was appropriate. Once courses were agreed upon, the faculty decided on a one-to-one exchange of course credit. The agreement between institutional faculties was the beginning of a long process to ensure that the student transfer of courses and credits was implemented.

Therefore, it was critical that the faculty work within each institutional structure (admissions, registrar, etc.) to ensure that the transfer of student work would not be under the general ECTS process but would be one-for-one, as agreed upon. This alleviates the need for students from UCL to take additional hours to make up for a loss of transfer credit, and thus they do not need to extend their time at Clemson to undertake coursework already mastered at their home institution.

Pedagogy

During these discussions, it was noted that all institutions do not have a common method of content delivery. This is of particular interest since the students in the program take upper division courses in their second language; Clemson students take advanced courses taught in French, and UCL students attend classes in English. Therefore, students must adjust to the language as well as teaching styles. Clemson holds classes in which professors traditionally deliver content through lectures, students participate in discussions and project presentations, and tests or examinations are held periodically. UCL classes do not engage students in testing prior to the end of the semester. The faculty are equally rigorous in expectations of content learned in courses, but the delivery of content is typically not via lectures but via assignments and challenges. Students take an examination at the end of the semester to demonstrate their knowledge, skills, and abilities but do not evaluate performance during the course of the semester. Clemson classrooms are more similar to UM classrooms than to UCL classrooms.

To help the Clemson students transition into an academic community with a new style of accountability and responsibility, the students attend pre-departure sessions covering the differences in academic cultures. Additionally, Clemson students visit the EU institutions prior to the exchange. While visiting, the students are introduced to their cohort fellows, allowing them opportunities to share their experiences both within the classroom and the academy at large. Additionally, the Clemson students are required to attend a pre-departure orientation session held by Clemson's Office of International Affairs. The session provides students with valuable information on safety, health, insurance, course registration, cultural adjustment, and other important topics related to pre-departure preparation, time abroad, and returning to Clemson. Peer interaction is a third method employed by the Economics Department to help the outbound students gain useful information, including hints regarding housing, shopping, and academic issues. Social events are provided, sharing in classes, and other opportunities allow students who are interested in travel to learn from those who have benefited from participating in the program.

General Education

*Workload:* Clemson is mandated to include general education courses or experiences as a part of the undergraduate program. For the UCL students, taking courses outside of their discipline is not typical. They must have completed all of the UCL requirements prior to arrival at Clemson and, in one academic year, complete all degree program requirements (including general education requirements) prior to their graduation. UCL students enroll in 18 or 19 hours of coursework to achieve the mandatory general education course credits as well as the economics courses.

*Foreign language:* As a rule, foreign language requirements for those majoring in economics are met through successful completion of French, Spanish, or other offered language courses. For the UCL students, enrolling in a French course would not meet the intent of the general education requirement, which is to acquire linguistic skills in a second language. The faculty of the Economics Department, with support from the Department of English, administer the SPEAK test, a part of the English as a Second Language program, to the UCL students. UCL students who pass this test receive credit for English as their foreign language. Passing the SPEAK test does not eliminate the requirement that UCL students take general education written or oral communication courses or literature courses taught in English. Overall, the UCL students must demonstrate their English language skills in all courses, since all lectures, resource materials, and testing are conducted in English. Similarly, the Clemson students perform in their second language, French, although this achievement does not fulfill a mandate for general education.

*Selecting general education courses:* Enrolling as seniors from UCL in Clemson freshmen classes such as biology and physics requires that the Clemson advisor be able to coordinate enrollment with the departments offering the courses. Clemson students enroll for fall courses in the spring or summer of the previous academic year. This enrollment calendar preempts the opportunity for incoming UCL students to sign up for classes, since they have not been formally admitted to Clemson. It is only upon completion of the transcript evaluation that the registration portal is open. Once the students are admitted, the advisor is able to assist in course enrollment. One challenge is that the transcript needs to be received by Clemson in the early spring. At that time, however, the EU students have not yet completed certain classes that they must pass. By making sure that the transcripts are sent from UCL to Clemson, a preliminary review can be made and the student enrollment process can begin much earlier than if it were necessary to wait until the completion of spring UCL courses.

*General education competencies in the discipline:* The Department of Economics is required to offer several general education competencies (e.g., ethics, professional development), and these are integrated into the required courses. Other courses offered by the department for the purpose of general education meet the science and technology requirement (but not the science lab course requirement). Because these courses are offered by the Department of Economics, the student advisor is able to work with the faculty to hold a given number of slots for the incoming cohort of UCL students. The cohort design allows students to be assured of enrollment in classes necessary for graduation.

## Summary

The TransAtlantic Exchange in Economics celebrated the graduation of the second cohort of students from Clemson in the spring of 2009. The program is founded on principles that are characteristic of many successful partnerships, including:

- Solutions to divergent program requirements must be *flexible* within the culture of the participating institutions.

- The departments must make *commitments* to the success of the program, so that it can be integrated, rather than dependent for success on the engagement of one faculty member.

- The importance of ongoing, extensive *faculty collaboration* is required both within an institution and between partner institutions.

- Attracting and maintaining qualified *students* whose lives will be enriched through the exchange process as well as the achievement of a dual degree from two prestigious institutions of higher learning is both critical and challenging.

The TREE program, developed by UCL and Clemson, exemplifies a dynamic model that continues to meet the dual degree needs of both the EU and U.S. institutions involved and to contribute to building EU-U.S. international educational cooperation.

# Transatlantic Degree Program – At a Glance

| Name of Program | TransAtlantic Exchange in Economics (TREE) | | | | | |
|---|---|---|---|---|---|---|
| Partner Institutions | Clemson University<br>Universite Catholique de Louvain<br>University Maastricht | | | | | |
| Location of Study | Clemson University, Clemson, SC, U.S. | | | | | |
| Academic Field(s) | Economics | | | | | |
| Academic Level | Undergraduate | | | | | |
| Year Started | 2006 | What type of degree is awarded? | | Double | | |
| Language(s) of Instruction | | English | | | | |
| How many students participated in the most recent year of the program? | | | | | | |
| | EU students | 12 | U.S. students | 7 | Other students | 0 |
| How many students have graduated from the program since it began? | | | | | | |
| | EU students | 7 | U.S. students | 0 | Other students | 0 |

# MAXIMIZING VALUES THROUGH THE ATLANTIS PROGRAM

BY EMERIC SOLYMOSSY AND PETER GUSTAVSSON

This article emerges from the experience of the authors as administrators involved in an innovative international collaborative dual degree program that began in 2007. The program, titled "Action for Transatlantic Links and Academic Networks for Training and Integrated Studies" (ATLANTIS), joins students from the United States, Sweden, and France in a multinational course of study resulting in two degrees: one from their home university, the other from one of the other two participating institutions. Unlike most international study exchange programs that allow for only one semester or one academic year abroad, this is a two-year program involving three countries. The first cohort of students studied at the Ecole de Commerce Européenne (ECE) in Lyon, France, in the fall semester of 2007. They continued their studies at Linköping University (LiU) in Linkoping, Sweden, during the spring semester of 2008. The cohort spent the fall semester of 2008 and the spring semester of 2009 in the United States at either Western Illinois University (Macomb or Moline, Illinois) or DePaul University (Chicago, Illinois).

The goals of this program are to enhance international understanding, promote personal growth, and increase students' global competitiveness. Institutionally, these goals are pursued by establishing personal and institutional partnerships that are sustainable over the long term. Students were actively recruited from the three participating countries. Each student was screened for academic performance, willingness to participate in the exchange program, and understanding of the program requirements.

Within the first few months of the exchange, however, numerous issues surfaced causing concern, including evidence of unsatisfactory academic performance. It seemed that academic performance, one of the principal measures being used to gauge the program's success, was not properly matched with participants' expectations and goals. Investigating the circumstances and likely causes of this issue led to a research project to explore the objectives, expectations, and realizations of this exchange program, with thoughts that the data might provide insight for similar programs. While this research is ongoing, enough data have been collected, coded, and analyzed to allow prescriptive suggestions for others. We are mindful that we are presenting these suggestions from the provider's perspective. They are based on research data and presented here in a distilled form.

As representatives of the participating universities began discussing the challenges they confronted, thoughts and observations were drawn on a large whiteboard. Value creation emerged as a central theme and, more specifically, representatives noted that all of the challenges were being framed in an input/output (cost/benefit, expected value) discourse. This led us to review accepted models of value creation and determination.

In spite of numerous theories of value creation (see Thompson, 1967, Normann & Ramirez, 1993, Stabell & Fjelstad, 1998, and Allee, 2003), there is no general consensus on a broadly applicable concept of value creation (Lepak et al., 2007) or on how value can be maximized for different stakeholders in a complex process. It is difficult to reach an agreement among researchers regarding what value creation really represents and how it is created (Lepak et al., 2007).

We separated the groups and inviduals involved in maintaining this program into three categories: facilitators, implementers, and students. We then gathered data regarding anticipated investment (considering both tangible and intangible resources valued by the persons), expected take-away value, and realized take-away value. We also gathered data regarding unanticipated costs or other difficulties encountered in the process. The researchers then began to conceive of the program's value in terms of a value *stream*: an analogy of value creation that incorporates elements of previous research into a practical model of value creation with ancillary losses and differential value systems. A river can be used as a metaphor for our value stream. In a river, water is known to have value. There are several sources of the water, with some more identifiable than others. As there are multiple sources of water, there are multiple uses, each of which also has value. The value attributed to the use of water is based on the unique needs of the user. Power generation, drinking, irrigation, and bathing each reflect valuable, yet distinctly different, uses. Furthermore, the structure and environment within which a river flows will contain many natural and dynamic opportunities for the flow of water to be altered, slowed, or lost (evaporation, absorption, and diversion). The river, therefore, will exhibit different levels of efficiency of value creation and delivery. We argue that the value creation process and the value stream exhibit comparable characteristics.

The following is a presentation of the key observations and recommendations emerging from our analysis of each of the three groups involved in the program—program facilitators, implementers, and students:

**Program facilitators** invest tangible resources to establish and promote exchange programs such as ours. Specifically, the U.S. Department of Education's Fund for the Improvement of Postsecondary Education (FIPSE) and the European Commission's Directorate General for Education and Culture jointly administer the EU-U.S. Atlantis Program, which provides grants for up to four years to add a European Community-United States dimension to international curriculum development and related student exchange. Our ATLANTIS program is only one of the many exchange programs funded annually through the larger EU-U.S. Atlantis Program.

In addition to providing startup funds for programs such as ours, program facilitators like FIPSE and the European Commission create intangible benefits that exceed the boundaries of the initial programs they fund. For instance, the ATLANTIS program at our institutions led to the research into value creation in exchange programs that made this article possible. This is similar to a river overflowing its banks or carving a channel due to heavy volumes of inflow. In regards to desired, tangible outcomes, the facilitators are less specific. An absence of articulated outcome expectations for any particular program might also be a result of its newness. Our recommendation is for program facilitators to carefully analyze projects funded through the EU-U.S. Atlantis Program on an annual basis and to compile a "best practices" list that can be shared with all participants. This will allow for the greatest distribution of excellence, increasing the effectiveness of the overall funding program.

**Implementers**—institutional administrators, project managers, and instructional faculty—should accept two critical ideas from the onset: a transatlantic joint and dual degree program is different than anything they've done in the past, and data strongly demonstrate that everything costs more and takes more time than anticipated. Although startup grants provide program funding, institutions also invest resources, which not only have tangible costs but also involve lost opportunity costs—time spent on grant activities cannot be used elsewhere. This was compounded by data indicating that the majority of program participants were involved because of an organizational imperative (function of the job, directed involvement, etc.) rather than personal or professional interest. Work is more effective and more efficient if fueled by passion rather than by command. Institutionally, it is necessary to provide support, including instructional support. Soliciting volunteers who want to be involved will likely lead to higher levels of personal commitment.

At the same time, there was a solid indication that volunteers would frequently seek side benefits or ancillary rewards that were not directly related to the program, such as personal travel or enhanced personal opportunities. All program participants entered the program with an expected value outcome. It is reasonable that they also seek cumulative values beyond the boundaries of the ATLANTIS program. Participants from the institutional quarter should, however, be reminded that the program's objectives extend beyond a "what's in it for me" perspective. It is acceptable to draw water from the river for personal use but unacceptable to remove a quantity for irrigating one's fields at the expense of downstream users.

Argyris and Schön (1974) called attention to differences between expressed and enacted values. A similar disconnect was manifested in student selection. Students were selected for inclusion in the program according to traditional institutional criteria: academic performance, willingness to participate in the exchange program, and expressed understanding of the program requirements. This assumes that academic performance is a principally sought outcome (which it was not), that willingness to participate is the same as cultural adaptability (which it is not), and that program requirements are articulated in sufficient detail as to permit informed agreement. The overriding goal of the ATLANTIS program at our institutions is enhanced understanding and cultural integration, which suggests that primary selection criteria should be students' sensitivity and adaptability rather than past academic achievement. These criteria, however, require a more intensive and subjective selection process.

While elements of the program requirements (the amount of funding and the necessity that students spend one semester in Lyon, France, one semester in Linköping, Sweden, and one academic year in the U.S.) were clearly articulated, certain critical aspects were not clear: course offerings and selection, attendance and participation requirements, assessment mechanisms, behavioral policies, and guidelines for non-program travel. This is like asking people to gather water out of a river. They have been told where in very general terms, and how much, but when they arrive at the river they are confronted with steep walls, rapids, and have the wrong container. The difficulties experienced in the first year of the program centered on issues that were poorly articulated. As a result, the second-year cohort of students was presented with more-defined course offerings, guidelines for personal conduct, clarified assessment parameters, and some guidelines for personal travel. Students, from the beginning, were more interested in international exposure than academic study. They sought to maximize experience while meeting only the established minimum to earn the coveted dual degree. The students' prioritized value system must be recognized by the administrators and project managers. Maximum expected value can only be achieved if the program is designed to specifically allow both academic achievement and personal experience. A versatile river allows for both hydroelectric generation and casual recreation. An international student exchange program with maximized value-stream processes should satisfy both the academic performance values of the program facilitators and the international experiences and recreation values of the students.

**Student** responses suggested many of their program objectives were being exceeded. The areas of take-away value that students cited most often were travel, self-development, cultural awareness, and language skills. Their academic objectives, however, were not satisfied as well. There is a paradox between the students' desired international exposure (differences) and their disappointment at things being different than expected or customary. Student responses reflected the effects of confusion due to newness of the program, tangible losses (time, internship, student loan, financial), and disappointment with the quality of the education. The program was not producing maximum value.

Students acknowledged that they were entering different educational systems with different instructional models and infrastructures. However, they frequently complained about the course scheduling, communication processes, grading procedures, and unavailability of educational materials. Students were not prepared for the magnitude of change they encountered. They were not prepared for difficulties in locating lodging, learning the transportation system, understanding scheduling communication procedures, or conducting financial transactions. These difficulties correlate to administrators expressing dismay at the amount of "hand-holding" required by the students. Both perspectives indicate deficiencies in logistics.

As a result of initial data, second-year students were provided with a one-week orientation experience through a structured "hunt game" with designated tasks (such as navigating buses, ordering food from a menu, taking photos of apartments, exchanging currency, locating the municipal registration office, and acquiring course schedules). This experience ensured that students had more realistic expectations of what they would encounter.

While the program must provide adequate logistical support to reduce uncertainty and student anxiety, students should not hold unrealistic expectations of a no-sacrifice experience. Students complained of opportunity costs (lost internship opportunities, delayed graduation, etc.) and financial inadequacies. Opportunity costs are identifiable prior to the participation agreement. Stipends are also identified. There were difficulties with stipends being denominated differently for European students (in euros) than for U.S. students (in U.S. dollars). The exchange rates resulted in European students' stipends being higher than U.S. students', which the latter saw as unfair. Students, knowing what their stipends would be, later complained of inadequate funding. This, however, was also attributed to lifestyle choices (e.g., choosing a private rather than shared apartment and pursuing personal travel). While self-serving behavior has already been mentioned, this issue may justify reinforcing the idea of "no free lunches" to students. Students might benefit from being required to articulate and record program benefits and costs through the orientation process.

Well into the second year, our ATLANTIS program is demonstrating positive results. Students, faculty, and administrative personnel are gaining experience, expressing increased understanding, and demonstrating more cross-cultural tolerance. Institutions are gaining international exposure and stature. Students and faculty are benefiting from globally integrated knowledge as well as expanded and enhanced networks.

## Discussion

Data from our experience yields prescriptive recommendations for improving not only this exchange program but also similar collaborations, principally in the areas of initiation and measurement. From an initiation perspective, there should be greater focus on articulating the intended outcome for all participants. The presumed value being passed downstream may not be valued by the recipient. For example, the courses themselves were presumed to be valuable by the providers; however, the students valued the personal interaction with other students more than the courses. The courses provided a vehicle for students to achieve their values but were not in themselves the valued item. Greater success may be realized by placing less emphasis on academic excellence and more emphasis on sensitivity to differences and cultural adaptability. Implementing enhanced cultural and country orientation (being more attentive but not "hand-holding") has direct, positive effects on students' perceived hardships and negativity, which, in turn, reduces conflict—cited as a hardship by several administrators, project managers, and instructors.

Through our project, we were able to develop meaningful, collaborative, and enduring research, focusing on value creation. The value stream model recognizes that providers pass elements downstream that they presume to have value, with the expectation that the recipients will value these elements to a comparable extent. This is not always the case. Both the program facilitators and students saw value in the dual degree combining business and technology. The providers, however, underestimated the value that students placed on non-academic experiences. The value stream model can be applied to other value-producing processes, offering the possibility to enhance existing theories. The value stream model also recognizes that value can be created outside of the initial expectations of the project. Our last prescription: all three groups should use exchanges such as our program to develop the kinds of opportunities they value, while keeping a flexible perspective on where additional opportunities may reside.

REFERENCES

Allee, V. (2003). *The future of knowledge: Increasing prosperity through value networks.* Burlington, MA: Butterworth-Heinemann.

Argyris, C., & Schön, D. (1974). *Theory in practice: Increasing professional effectiveness.* San Francisco: Jossey-Bass Publishers.

Lepak, D.P., Smith, K.G., & Taylor, M.S. (2007). Value creation and value capture: A multilevel perspective. *Academy of Management Review, 32/1*, 180-194.

Normann, R., & Ramírez, R. (1993). From value chain to value constellation: Designing interactive strategy. *Harvard Business Review, 71*, 65-77.

Stabell, C.B., & Fjeldstad, O. (1998). Configuring value for competitive advantage: On chains, shops, and networks. *Strategic Management Journal, 19*.

Thompson, J.D. (1967). *Organizations in action.* New York: McGraw Hill.

# Transatlantic Degree Program – At a Glance

| | |
|---|---|
| Name of Program | Transatlantic Links and Academic Networks for Training and Integrated Studies (ATLANTIS) |
| Partner Institutions | Western Illinois University (Macomb and Moline, IL, U.S.) DePaul University (Chicago, IL, U.S.) Linköping University (Linköping, Sweden) Ecole de Commerce Europeenne (Lyon, France) |
| Location of Study | 1$^{st}$ Semester: Lyon, France. 2$^{nd}$ Semester: Linköping, Sweden. 3$^{rd}$ and 4$^{th}$ Semesters: Either Macomb, Moline, or Chicago, Illinois, U.S. |
| Academic Field(s) | Business and Information Technology |
| Academic Level | Upper Division, Bachelor's |

| Year Started | 2007 | What type of degree is awarded? | Double |
|---|---|---|---|

| Language(s) of Instruction | English |
|---|---|

| How many students participated in the most recent year of the program? | | | | | |
|---|---|---|---|---|---|
| | EU students | 12 | U.S. students | 10 | Other students | |

| How many students have graduated from the program since it began? | | | | | |
|---|---|---|---|---|---|
| | EU students | 12 | U.S. students | 4 | Other students | |

# A Unique Exchange Program for Mechanical Engineering Students at the Milwaukee School of Engineering and the Fachhochschule Lübeck

By John E. Pakkala, Jürgen E. Blechschmidt,
Joseph C. Musto, Hans H. Reddemann
Revised edition by Jürgen E. Blechschmidt[*]

An exchange program for mechanical engineering students has been implemented between the Milwaukee School of Engineering in Milwaukee (MSOE), Wisconsin, United States, and the University of Applied Sciences Lübeck (Fachhochschule Lübeck, or FHL), Germany. This International Mechanical Engineering program (ISM) requires participants to spend two semesters abroad, and curricula have been thoroughly designed so students earn Bachelor of Science degrees from both universities in the usual four-year time span.

The program requires students to spend their first two years at the home institution. All students spend the third year of the program in Lübeck, and the fourth year is completed in Milwaukee. These last two years comprise the portion of the program that both German and American students spend together. All students must also complete an undergraduate diploma thesis (*Diplomarbeit*) related to their year-long senior design project. As of 2009, three cohorts of mechanical engineering students have successfully graduated from the program at MSOE.

## Background

Many factors and needs have prompted the creation of the program, including input from industry, international engineering education standardization efforts, the Bologna Accord (see http://europa.eu/index_en.htm, National Science Foundation, 2006, & Narula and Duysters, 2004), the Pan American Federation of Engineering Societies (UPADI), and others.

---

[*] This article is a revised edition of the authors' contribution to the 7th Annual ASEE Global Colloquium on Engineering Education, Cape Town, South Africa, October 19-23, 2008.

International collaboration, if poorly orchestrated, can have deleterious effects. For example, poor communication between engineering departments in different countries led to Airbus A380 production delays and attendant stock devaluation (Robertson, 2006). Perhaps Continental AG, in its final report on the global engineering excellence initiative (see www.conti-online.com) put it most succinctly: "Transnational mobility for engineering students, researchers, and professionals needs to become a priority."

Universities have implemented a wide variety of international study and exchange programs for both students and faculty (Polczynski, 2006, & Jones, 2006). However, many programs suffer from curricular constraints that do not allow students to earn full credit at the home university for courses taken abroad or to take enough courses that are applicable to their degrees. The program outlined here provides seamless transfer of credit in both directions. The curriculum was designed so that students complete their dual degree program in a four-year time span.

The program also offers the participating universities the opportunity to explore the inherent properties of educational programs that span linguistic and cultural lines. This program along with other similar programs could also facilitate efforts toward international standardization of engineering programs (Buckeridge, 2000).

## Participating Institutions

Founded in 1903, Milwaukee School of Engineering (www.msoe.edu) offers 17 bachelor's degree programs and 10 master's degree programs in engineering, engineering technology, business, communication, construction management, medical informatics, nursing, and perfusion. MSOE faculty are passionate about teaching, and that is their main focus. Many come to the university with varied experiences working in industry, bringing their practical knowledge to the classroom. Small class sizes keep instructors in close contact with students. Most of the courses are geared toward experience-based learning with professors responsible for and supervising laboratory experiments. MSOE does not use teaching assistants.

The Fachhochschule Lübeck (www.fh-luebeck.de), a University of Applied Sciences, is founded on 200 years of tradition and expertise in education. FHL provides many centers of competence, including entrepreneurship, polymer science, hydrogen technology, and others. FHL was also one of the founding universities and leading proponents of a € 22 million project to create an e-learning platform for undergraduate learning in Germany (see www.oncampus.de). One of FHL's main objectives is "applied science in cooperation with third parties and industry." FHL is the leading university of applied sciences in Germany in this area. Competence in teaching is considered the lifeblood of the institution.

FHL and MSOE both regard applied science as a central focus of their education, their research, and their common self-understanding and missions. In 1995, MSOE and FHL began their cooperation in this area with an international double degree program in electrical engineering. In 2005 the International Mechanical Engineering program (abbreviated ISM following the German) was established.

## Program Objectives of the ISM

The ISM program aims to achieve specific objectives for the following groups:

<u>Students</u>

- Offer the opportunity for a student to earn a degree from both participating universities.

- Enable students to get different learning experiences at a typical German and North American university.

- Enable students to receive insight into country-specific ways of life and value systems.

- Let students gain competence in two different languages and their uses in two different fields—business and engineering.

<u>Faculty</u>

- Enable faculty members to experience the differences in behavior, learning styles, and skills of students from different cultures.

- Allow faculty members to learn from each other in the same way as students through an instructor exchange program.

<u>Institutions</u>

- The two universities experience not only different technical approaches but even philosophical, ethical, and other fields of cooperation.

<u>Industry</u>

- The cooperation of the universities creates a strong international link between graduates, enabling long-term collaboration.

- The program allows American, German, and multinational companies to develop special relations with the local university.

<u>All Parties Involved</u>

- The international cooperation program helps to strengthen cooperation among all three groups: students, the two universities, and local industry.

- This cooperation creates many benefits for all three parties and enables productive strategic partnerships.

## Senior Capstone Design and the Diploma Thesis

Two highlights of the program are the capstone design project at MSOE and the diploma thesis (*Diplomarbeit*) from FHL, which are both mandatory. The capstone project spans the student's senior academic year in Milwaukee; the diploma thesis takes place during the final three months and contains an in-depth, independent investigation of one or several aspects pertinent to the student's senior design project. The nature of the group design projects allows participants to gain valuable team experience. The diploma thesis portion of the program also enables students to hone their own independent research, design, and analysis skills.

Common objectives:

- The ability to realize and evaluate designs; to identify, formulate, model, and solve engineering problems.

- The ability to design and select components and processes for mechanical and thermal systems; to serve an engineering function on a design team, involving the design of a complex system under real-world constraints (i.e., environmental, cost, safety, manufacturing, etc.).

- An understanding of engineering as a professional pursuit.

- The ability to solve technical problems with limited resources and within a limited time, and to write scientific reports and give technical presentations.

- The prediction of design results and proving of experimental data using accepted theory.

The FHL *Diplomarbeit* carries a heavy weight (30 percent of the total credits) on the final FHL grade point average and provides the "masterpiece experience" in German education. Additionally, each participant defends his or her individually prepared diploma thesis before a panel of FHL and MSOE faculty at the end of the fourth year.

However, current constraints inherent in the MSOE system limit the combined weight of the capstone design and diploma thesis works to less than 10 percent of the final MSOE grade point average. This creates a motivation imbalance among students from the two countries: German students exhibit a high level of motivation due to their understanding of the value of the thesis with respect to employment opportunities in their home country. American students understand that their grade on the thesis is quite likely not of prime importance to American employers—and that their general international experience may carry more weight. Currently, at MSOE American students are encouraged to understand this motivational difference and approach the diploma thesis with the idea that their FHL degree is dependent upon the thesis, and their performance may influence employment abroad, especially in Europe. Students are counseled that earning two degrees in four years requires more work, regardless of the credit tally at the time of graduation.

## Accreditation

### MSOE

In the United States, many undergraduate education programs in mechanical engineering are accredited by a procedure carried out by the Accreditation Board for Engineering and Technology (ABET) (see www.abet.org). MSOE grants ABET-accredited Bachelor of Science in Mechanical Engineering (BScME) degrees.

The international exchange program faces two related but distinct challenges from an accreditation standpoint:

- Validating that MSOE students spending their third year at FHL meet all of the requirements of the accredited BScME program.

- Validating that the FHL students spending their fourth year at MSOE meet the program requirements at MSOE.

The former challenge is more a matter of documentation; MSOE students who spend their third year at FHL directly meet all existing curricular requirements for the accredited BScME. Through careful maintenance of syllabi, close coordination between faculty members across institutions, and through collection of student sample work, one can claim and demonstrate that the coursework completed by MSOE students while in residence at FHL is equivalent to the coursework that would be done at MSOE.

The latter challenge is a more difficult one. Students from FHL spend only one year in residence at MSOE but are granted an ABET-accredited BScME at the conclusion of the program. The strategy for demonstrating that these students meet all program requirements is two-pronged:

- Demonstrating that the coursework completed by students at FHL is topically equivalent to MSOE coursework. That is, demonstrating that the coursework both prepared the students for achieving the outcomes of the BScME program at MSOE and met the ABET minimum topical requirements.

- Integrating the students from FHL into the outcomes assessment plan of the program in order to assure that students are meeting the program outcomes at a satisfactory level.

Beyond curricular mapping, integration of the FHL students into the outcomes assessment process was seen as a key component in approaching accreditation requirements. Assessment integration was achieved in two ways:

- As part of the assessment plan at MSOE, comprehensive, objectively scored examinations are given in the basic mechanics sequence (statics, dynamics, and mechanics of materials). These examinations have been periodically shared and administered to FHL students in their basic mechanics courses and the results shared with MSOE faculty for assessment purposes.

- FHL students participate in the capstone design sequence at MSOE. During this sequence, two assessment instruments are used to evaluate all students with respect to the program outcomes and objectives. In addition, program-specific accreditation requirements are further assured by mandating that FHL students take design/realization courses in both mechanical and thermal systems while at MSOE.

FHL

In Germany, the accreditation of study programs originally was carried out by the ministry of education in the respective province. The degree granted by FHL is currently a *Diplom-Ingenieur* (FH), based on a four-year program. This degree enables graduates at once to work as professional engineers in Germany, Europe, and worldwide. It must be mentioned that the procedure will change to be handled by accreditation agencies in the near future based on the Bologna declaration (see http://europa.eu/index_en.htm).

## Status of the Program

Teaching Experience

The complete program in Germany is delivered in the English language by FHL professors. The language question created an opportunity to learn more about the local teaching staff at FHL; it became apparent very quickly which faculty members were willing and able to conduct classes in a language other than their mother tongue. Several teachers' meetings in advance of the first cohort of students created a new kind of common culture with some identification with the program on the side of the professors.

The students came together very quickly to start their own "ISM world." Strong team identification and micro-socialization began to occur—first among the students, but later even among the professors.

During oral defense meetings at MSOE, new contact arose between MSOE and FHL professors, even those only peripherally involved in the program. These contacts continue to develop and are very promising.

Quarter System versus Semester System

MSOE operates on a yearly schedule of three academic quarters beginning in early September and running through late May. Students are accustomed to a typically "American" process of education: a strongly regulated schedule that safely guides them through the study program utilizing periodic testing, quizzes, and lab report submittals. This is in stark contrast to the German model of largely unsupervised instruction and a single exam at the end of the semester. The FHL study program plan follows a schedule of two semesters per year, starting in September and ending in July the following year.

The credit conversion system was designed to offer seamless transfer of credit from courses completed in Lübeck to the degree tracks of both FHL and MSOE. Similarly, German students completing their fourth year in Milwaukee can apply all courses completed in Milwaukee to both degrees. To date, no major problems have arisen concerning scheduling differences in the quarter versus semester system, because a whole year is spent abroad. Some academic details or learning methods have been problematic for some students as they adjust to the different examination methods and schedules. It is not clear whether these problems are associated with the program or if those particular students would exhibit similar problems in any case.

The program is generally considered very successful, but it is not without problems. One problem regarding balancing the course load in Milwaukee has surfaced. During winter quarter of their fourth year German students face a heavy load of courses, many involving reading and writing English (which is, of course, not their native language and often technical, involving specialized vocabulary used in either social sciences or health sciences). One solution to this problem is to invite MSOE professors to teach a course in Lübeck for third-year German participants, thus reducing their schedule overload the following year. Of course, this increases the load during the third year, but students have indicated that the trade-off is a good one.

Faculty Exchange

So far, three faculty members have participated in an exchange program by teaching abroad at the partner university. Two MSOE professors conducted "American-style" courses in Lübeck, and one FHL professor gave a two-week-long workshop in Milwaukee. Students participating in these courses were thus informed about the teaching style of the partner university in advance, easing their transition to the new system. Faculty members gained insight into how their own teaching style affects students who are unaccustomed to their particular approach. Student feedback has been very positive regarding courses taught under this faculty exchange.

In addition to providing a cultural experience for both students and professors, the faculty exchange is an effective tool for maintaining curricular focus and accreditation. Faculty colleagues share topical information in specific courses, facilitating seamless transfer of students into subsequent related courses. The firsthand knowledge of the partner university gained through the faculty exchange permits a higher level of confidence from both universities in granting degrees.

## Conclusions and General Observations

Several important results are evident from our experience of the program so far:

- The universities and the students benefit greatly. The program yields rewards much greater than the sum of its constituent parts—which might be expressed mathematically as follows: $(1 + 1) \gg 2$

- Development of this program has provided MSOE and FHL with valuable information in many areas, including thesis preparation requirements, cross-cultural course content, and national education system similarities and differences.

- Some evidence suggests intrinsic differences due to the differing tuition structures. Students paying much higher tuition in the United States may occasionally expect more personal attention from faculty members than their counterparts who pay a comparatively low fee. This tuition gap may also affect the teaching styles at the two universities. However, faculty exchange experiences indicate that personal attention differences among international colleagues are no larger than the differences inherently present among any group of higher education officials. Students can sometimes view differences as institutional rather than attributing them to a preferred teaching style.

- The people at each institution who are responsible for administration are very important to the success of the program. Faculty members are critical to the academic health of the exchange, which extends to accreditation issues. Administration officials provide students with a smooth transition to a new culture by offering information on visas, banking, housing, matriculation, and the many other details associated with the initial phases of the experience.

- The program has proven itself to be a very effective recruiting tool for both universities.

- Of the German students who have completed the program, two have taken employment offers in the United States. Until now, none of the American students have taken jobs abroad, but some are going to continue in graduate programs in Germany.

In fall 2009, the fifth generation of mechanical engineering students began their common program in Lübeck. Meanwhile, three cohorts of ISM students have already successfully graduated from the program. We expect to continue to refine the program in subsequent years.

---

REFERENCES

Buckeridge, J.S. (2000). Y2K imperative: The globalisation of engineering education. *Global Journal of Engineering Education, 4/1*, 19-24.

Jones, R.C. (2006). *Continuing education for faculty members in developing countries.* Proceedings of the 10th IACEE World Conference on Continuing Education. Retrieved August 10, 2009 from http://www.iacee.org/wccee/2006/index.html.

Narula, R. & Duysters, G. (2004). Globalisation and trends in international R&D alliances. *Journal of International Management, 10/2*, 199-218.

National Science Foundation. (2006). *Science and engineering indicators 2006.* Accessed May 2008 from www.nsf.gov/statistics/seind06/c6/c6s1.htm.

Polczynski, M. (2006). *Expanding extracurricular learning opportunities through international engineering student and faculty exchange.* Retrieved August 10, 2009 from www.nciia.org/conf_06/papers/pdf/polczynski.pdf.

Robertson, D. (2006, October 4). EADS slumps on €4.8bn Airbus delays *The Times Online.* Retrieved from http://business.timesonline.co.uk.

## Transatlantic Degree Program – At a Glance

| | | | | | |
|---|---|---|---|---|---|
| Name of Program | International Studies Mechanical Engineering (ISM) | | | | |
| Partner Institutions | University of Applied Sciences Lübeck (FHL), Germany<br>Milwaukee School of Engineering, Wisconsin, U.S. | | | | |
| Location of Study | Lübeck, Germany and Milwaukee, U.S. | | | | |
| Academic Field(s) | Mechanical Engineering | | | | |
| Academic Level | Undergraduate (= Dipl.-Ing. & Bachelor of Science) | | | | |
| Year Started | 2005 | What type of degree is awarded? | | Double | |
| Language(s) of Instruction | | English and German | | | |
| How many students participated in the most recent year of the program? | | | | | |
| | EU students | 7 | U.S. students | 12 | Other students | 0 |
| How many students have graduated from the program since it began? | | | | | |
| | EU students | 12 | U.S. students | 14 | Other students | 0 |

# THE JUNIATA-BOCHOLT TRANSATLANTIC DOUBLE DEGREE IN INTERNATIONAL MANAGEMENT

BY JENIFER CUSHMAN

Establishing and then sustaining transatlantic double degree initiatives can be complicated, even frustrating. Certainly, the benefits for the students ultimately justify the expenditure of resources and energy needed to maintain such programs, but their success depends on a commitment from all partners at both the departmental and administrative levels. Business students at Juniata College in Pennsylvania can take advantage of a double degree program in international management with the Fachhochschule (FH; University of Applied Sciences) Gelsenkirchen in Bocholt, Germany, for example. This program allows students from either Juniata or Bocholt to receive two bachelor's degrees: a bachelor of arts from Juniata and a baccalaureate from FH-Gelsenkirchen Bocholt. The success of this program rests on the personal relationships formed at the departmental level as much as on the flexibility at the institutional level.

Founded in 1876, Juniata is an independent, private, coeducational, undergraduate college of liberal arts and sciences located in central Pennsylvania. The commitment to educate students to live responsibly in the world is a hallmark of Juniata, whose mission is to "provide an engaging personalized educational experience empowering our students to develop the skills, knowledge and values that lead to a fulfilling life of service and ethical leadership in the global community." Close to 40 percent of its approximately 1,500 students engage in an international experience, and the college is fortunate to enjoy a relatively large number of long-term international exchange relationships.

Students coming to Juniata from any of our exchange partners have long been able to take advantage of our partner degree offering, whereby students are awarded two degrees upon the completion of their studies at their home institution: the degree awarded by the home institution and a bachelor's degree from Juniata. In order to receive the partner degree, students must enter Juniata with the equivalent of at least 85 credits and complete the requisite number of credits in their major area of study, as well as a number of courses from across the curriculum including interdisciplinary cultural analysis that account for the liberal arts component of the Juniata degree.

Although Juniata has offered this partner degree option to our exchange students for many years, the reciprocal double degree is a more recent development. Juniata alumnus and trustee Dr. Christoph Schwemmlein, who lives and works in the Bocholt region, initiated the partnership between Juniata and the FH-Gelsenkirchen Bocholt in 2003. Founded in 1961 as a state engineering school, the FH-Gelsenkirchen adopted its current structure and name in 1992. Since then, the Business Department at the Bocholt campus has developed emphases on an international orientation and a practically based education.

The partnership between the two institutions was a natural one, in part because Juniata and Bocholt are both small institutions relatively far from urban centers. In both institutions, the emphasis on teaching excellence and supportive relationships between students and staff ensures a nurturing atmosphere for students. As an exclusively undergraduate institution, Juniata began the partnership with an eye to bachelor-level degrees. The Bologna process has facilitated the logistics of the partner degree program in that Juniata students enroll in Bocholt for the second semester of their junior year and first semester their senior year, but they actually come into the second semester, second year of courses in Bocholt's Bachelor's of International Management program. Juniata students thus enter the Bocholt course of study with roughly the same level of preparation as their German counterparts.

The first step towards collaboration between the two institutions was for the respective business departments to compare degree requirements and synthesize their curricula. Naturally, in order for faculty members to discuss curricular terms, they must be able to meet face-to-face. Double degree initiatives are almost impossible to implement without travel support both for administrative staff and faculty. Fortunately, Juniata budgets for the international travel necessary to maintain its many exchange relationships; at least seven Juniata faculty and staff have been able to visit Bocholt since its inception, including Juniata's president, provost, and Center for International Education (CIE) staff. Two business faculty members from each institution were able to visit the other during the program start-up.

Once the business faculties began comparing curricular models, the partner degree was established relatively quickly. The early involvement of academic staff in a specific field enabled the project to begin with little delay. Because of the decentralized structure of many European universities, U.S. institutions do well to focus initially on only one or two academic areas when establishing a double degree with a European partner. The "bottom-up" approach will reap the quickest rewards, as disparate academic divisions in European institutions tend to function relatively autonomously, and sometimes even run their own international offices independently of the larger institution.

One potential obstacle to maintaining a dynamic double degree exchange program is language. While the German students in the Bocholt international management track were generally proficient enough in English to jump into courses at Juniata, fewer Juniata business students had German proficiency. This obstacle was overcome by scheduling the first semester of Juniata students entering the Bocholt program to coincide with the all-English semester of the Bocholt international management track. Juniata students thus take an entire semester of English-language business courses in Germany while learning intensive German and before enrolling in German-language business courses.

Juniata students must complete two and a half years at Juniata before entering what corresponds to the fourth semester of the Bachelor's of International Management program at Bocholt. They thus spend the second semester of their junior year and the first semester of their senior year in Bocholt. By the end of their second semester at Bocholt, they must have written a bachelor's thesis, graded by a professor at FH-Gelsenkirchen Bocholt. They then return to Juniata for their final semester. Upon successful completion of their Juniata studies, students who received a passing grade on their Bocholt thesis receive both degrees at graduation.

Bocholt students must complete their first four semesters of the Bachelor's in International Management before entering Juniata, with at least 90 credits transferred from Bocholt. During their two semesters at Juniata, they must enroll in a total of 30 credits, with at least 14 of those within the Accounting, Business, and Economics Departments. In keeping with the liberal arts spirit of Juniata, students must also complete at least six credits outside of their major area of study and fulfill all other Juniata senior-year graduation requirements. They return to Bocholt for their sixth-semester courses; upon successful completion of their degree at Bocholt, students who have fulfilled the double degree requirements receive degrees from both institutions.

The above terms are the result of careful deliberations on the part of business professors. The reward is a vibrant exchange of students between the institutions and increasingly multifaceted collegial relationships between the two departments. Similarities in institutional size and pedagogic philosophies, coupled with flexible administrative policies, have also contributed to the success of the program. Juniata has hosted a Bocholt student every year of the program, and a total of five Bocholt students and two Juniata students have earned the partner degree since 2003. Students who have participated from both sides appreciate the value of building joint U.S. and EU credentials.

Although the partners have not yet undertaken a formal impact evaluation of the program, the partnership has been so successful that the two institutions are in the process of threshing out the particulars of a 3+2 master's program, whereby Juniata students would spend a total of six semesters at Juniata and four semesters at Bocholt, after which they would receive a bachelor's degree from Juniata and a master's degree in management from Bocholt. This could prove to be a particularly appealing recruiting tool for Juniata, which is exclusively an undergraduate institution. Other potential benefits of the program include the development of faculty exchanges (which would enable members of each department to become intimately familiar with the other's curricular and degree structures), mutual enrollment in summer workshops hosted by each institution, and the possibility to involve a third European partner in a transatlantic degree consortium in order to pursue funds for faculty and student mobility through the EU-U.S. Atlantis Program.

# Transatlantic Degree Program – At a Glance

| Name of Program | Juniata-Bocholt Double Degree | | |
|---|---|---|---|
| Partner Institutions | Juniata College, Huntingdon, PA, U.S.<br>Fachhochschule Gelsenkirchen-Bocholt, Germany | | |
| Location of Study | Huntingdon, PA, U.S. and Bocholt, Germany | | |
| Academic Field(s) | Business Management | | |
| Academic Level | Bachelor's | | |
| Year Started | 2003 | What type of degree is awarded? | Double |
| Language(s) of Instruction | | English & German | |
| How many students participated in the most recent year of the program? | | | |
| | EU students | 1 | U.S. students | 0 | Other students | |
| How many students have graduated from the program since it began? | | | |
| | EU students | 5 | U.S. students | 2 | Other students | |

# ELEVATING EXISTING STUDY PROGRAMS THROUGH THE INTEGRATION OF DOUBLE DEGREES: THE DOUBLE MASTER IN BUSINESS ADMINISTRATION AT THE UNIVERSITY OF COLOGNE

BY CHRISTI DEGEN AND CARSTEN KLENNER

## Background and Strategic Objectives

Founded in 1388, the University of Cologne comprises six faculties and is one of the largest public universities in Germany today. The Cologne Faculty of Management, Economics and Social Sciences currently accommodates more than 8,800 students in 14 study programs. Over its long history it has established an excellent academic reputation and developed affiliations with leading international institutions in business and academia. With the implementation of the Bologna reforms, the faculty has recently moved from traditional German diploma study programs to a two-cycle system with bachelor's and master's degrees.

The new two-year Master of Science in Business Administration stands out as one of our flagship programs. With the introduction of the new system we have been looking for ways to sharpen the profile of the master's program by providing additional options for highly ambitious students to internalize their course of study. Several alternatives were evaluated as a potential complement to the faculty's well-established one-semester exchange programs. An analysis revealed that an integration of double degrees into our existing master's program would provide the best fit with our strategic objectives. With such an integrated approach, the legal and organizational structures are created *within* the existing master's program in business administration, instead of implementing an additional and separate legal and organizational infrastructure for a double or joint degree. In the integrated approach the double degree is positioned and offered as an additional option for prospective master's students in the existing business administration program. Figure 1 provides an overview of the advantages from the two main stakeholders' perspectives.

FIGURE 1: PERCEIVED ADVANTAGES OF AN INTEGRATED DOUBLE MASTER PROGRAM

| Institutional perspective | Students' perspective |
| --- | --- |
| Academic value added: enrich own competence portfolio by specializations of top-ranked partner institutions | Extended choice: draw from the course portfolios and specializations of both institutions |
| Premium image effect: increase the attractiveness of the existing master's program and appeal to the highly qualified and ambitious students in the domestic and international markets | Career advantage: gain access to foreign labor markets, differentiate oneself with proven skills and competencies for an international work environment |
| Contribute to the internationalization strategy: strengthen the international orientation of program portfolio as one of the key differentiating factors from the domestic competition | International exposure and experience: obtain important cultural competencies, global adaptability and language skills |

## Program Development

At present, two bilateral Double Master programs have been implemented: the first one with the Louvain School of Management, Université Catolique de Louvain in Belgium, and the second one with the Helsinki School of Economics in Finland. Two more programs with partner institutions in Eastern Europe and two with non-European partners are currently under development. The integration of the double degree into the regular business administration master's program allows students to complete two master's degrees in business administration in the course of one single study program. One degree is issued by the University of Cologne and the other is issued by the partner institution. The students enrolled in the two-year Double Master program spend one year at home and one year at the partner institution. Drawing from the knowledge and specialization areas of two institutions from two different countries enables the students to sharpen their competency profile with additional academic and social skills. In the following paragraphs, we describe the program development for the double degree with the Louvain School of Management. Courses at the Louvain School of Management are taught in French and English, courses at the University of Cologne are taught in German and English. The instruments and implemented structures for the double degree with Louvain served as a solid basis for the development of further double degrees with other partner institutions.

As we chose to integrate the double degree into the existing master's program in business administration, the legal and organizational structures had to be created *within* the existing programs at both partner institutions. Thus, the overall legal and organizational framework required for the program did not have to be created entirely from scratch. This turned out to be an important advantage, leading to significant savings in overhead costs for the implementation and operation of the program. However, the existing master's programs in business administration at both institutions had been designed as self-contained entities that did not allow for a straightforward credit transfer recognition system (such as the European Credit Transfer and Accumulation System or ECTS) as is typically required for the implementation of a double degree in cooperation with a foreign partner institution. Though the master's programs at the two institutions encompass a total of 120 credit points and a two-year standard period of study, they expose a different structure (see Figure 2).

FIGURE 2: STRUCTURE OF THE REGULAR MASTER'S PROGRAMS AT THE PARTNER INSTITUTIONS (AS OF JANUARY 2006, WHEN THE FIRST NEGOTIATIONS WERE INITIATED)

| Cologne | | Louvain | |
|---|---|---|---|
| Master of Science in Business Administration | | Maître en sciences de gestion | |
| Methods and Techniques | 18 ECTS | Advanced Management | 30 ECTS |
| Major (1 of 5) | 54 ECTS | Specialization (1 of 13) | 30 ECTS |
| | | Elective (1 of 13) | 30 ECTS |
| Minor (1 of 31) | 24 ECTS | CSR Course or Internship | 10 ECTS |
| Master's Thesis | 24 ECTS | Master's Thesis | 20 ECTS |
| Total | 120 ECTS | Total | 120 ECTS |

The necessary condition for awarding a double degree in this context is that the students must fulfill the study regulations of both degrees. The main challenge was therefore to develop a program structure for the Double Master that would cover these regulations at both partner institutions to the greatest extent as possible. Changes in regulations needed to be minimized because they would also affect the regular master's degree programs at both institutions, which could potentially result in running into legal obstacles. A breakthrough in the discussions was achieved when participants had the idea to credit the core elements of one regular master's program as elective elements in the other master's program. The Double Master would then consist of the core elements in Cologne plus the core elements in Louvain plus an additional jointly supervised master's thesis. A potential increase in the overall workload compared to the regular master's programs was perceived as acceptable. As the workload for the regular master's programs represents an average workload depending on individual learning speed, the highly qualified students that the Double Master program targets would still be able to finish their studies in two years. In fact, the higher workload helps to position the Double Master as an ambitious program that is clearly distinguished from the regular master's programs. Based on these premises, a credit transfer scheme was negotiated and incorporated into a formal cooperation agreement that was signed by the two parties. Figure 3 provides an overview of the program structure, including the credit transfer paths to both institutions.

| Credit Transfer to Cologne | Extra Workload | Program Element | Extra Workload | Credit Transfer to Louvain |
|---|---|---|---|---|
| 18 | 0 | Methods & Techniques (UoC) 18 ECTS | 18 | 0 |
| 42 | 0 | Major-Core Courses (UoC) 42 ECTS | 2 | 40 |
| 12 | 18 | Advanced Management (UCL) 30 ECTS | 0 | 30 |
| 24 | 6 | Spezialisation (UCL) 30 ECTS | 0 | 30 |
| 24 | 0 | Thesis (UCL/UoC) 24 ECTS | 4 | 20 |

Totaling 60 ECTS credits, the integration of the program elements "Advanced Management" and "Specialization" provided by the Louvain School of Management could be accomplished in a straightforward way, without modification of the module structure. The modules "Methods & Techniques" and "Major" delivered by the Cologne Faculty of Management, Economics and Social Sciences turned out to be a little bit more difficult to integrate due to the total number of 72 credits. A deeper analysis of the curriculum in Cologne revealed that all five majors offered in Cologne could be broken up into a group of subject-specific "core courses" and more generally oriented "related courses." These "major-core courses" account for 42 credits. Adding the 18 credits from the module "Methods & Techniques," the program elements delivered in Cologne also accumulate up to 60 credits. In order to fulfill the study regulations in Cologne that the students have to complete 54 credits in their majors, 12 credits for the "related courses" are transferred from the module "Advanced Management" taught in Louvain. Twenty-four credits from the module "Specialization" taken in Louvain are credited as the "Minor" in Cologne. In Louvain, the credits from the "Major" taken in Cologne are transferred to "Elective" and "CSR Course or Internship." The partner institutions agreed on the stricter regulations for the master's thesis employed at the Cologne Faculty of Management, Economics and Social Sciences. Consequently, the jointly supervised master's thesis is credited with 24 credits. Moreover, the implementation of joint supervision procedures fosters intra-organizational collaboration and nurtures further cooperation activities in research and teaching.

## Organizational Implementation and Outlook

The implementation of the Double Master required a great deal of coordination, not only with the partner institution but also with internal stakeholders. The decentralized structure of the University of Cologne, which is very typical for a German public university, requires that many people need to be involved in discussions and the decision-making process. The project and program management was carried out by the International Relations Center of the Cologne Faculty of Management, Economics and Social Sciences, which is in charge of coordinating the faculty's international activities and possesses a wealth of experience in international cooperation activities.

According to our experiences, a phase-oriented plan proved to be successful in coping with, on the one hand, the conflicting requirements of flexibility for internal coordination, and on the other hand, the strong commitments for external communication with the partner institution. As a first major step, the university presidents and deans signed a letter of intent that outlined the strategic objectives and conditions of the planned double degree. The letter of intent proved extremely useful in the subsequent internal discussions. It emphasized the support and willingness of the partner institutions' management and directed internal discussions toward problem solving. A year later, an official cooperation agreement was signed as the second major step. The agreement delineated the legal and organizational structures to be implemented by the partner institutions (e.g., the credit transfer scheme). The implementation involved the modification of admission procedures and examination regulations. In order to avoid a major redesign of the examination regulations in Cologne, a shortcut was employed by creating an additional minor that serves as a black box for crediting the courses completed in Louvain. Additional transfer rules on a course basis were negotiated and approved separately with each person in charge for one of the five "Majors." The additional transfer rules facilitate the credit transfer of the "related course" taken in Louvain to the "Major" in Cologne.

Two alternative ways to enter the program have been established. The first way is to apply directly for the Double Master program at one of the partner institutions. For students who are enrolled in the regular master's program in business administration, it is also possible to apply for the Double Master program during their first study year. The application process is conducted in two rounds. After a first written application round, the candidates are shortlisted for personal interviews. The selection committee consists of two professors from the faculty admissions committee, two student representatives from the partner university, the international relations director, and the program coordinator.

## Outlook: A Transatlantic Perspective

After the successful launch of the Double Master in Business Administration with our European partners, we are now working intensively on the extension of the Double Master programs, in particular with partner institutions from North America and Asia.

Additional complexity is introduced when one goes beyond the European Higher Education Area, with its common basis of mutual degree recognition and credit transfer instigated by the Bologna Declaration. In the following checklist (see Figure 4) we highlight the key points for transatlantic double degrees that we have identified so far in discussions with interested stakeholders and potential partners in North America.

FIGURE 4: CHECKLIST FOR KICKING OFF TRANSATLANTIC DOUBLE DEGREES

| **Identify the value added from a student's perspective** |
| --- |
| What program at your partner institution is of most interest to your students? |
| What are the most compelling specialization areas being offered? |
| Which unique competencies and expertise can be provided by the partner institution that your institution does not have? |

| **Construct a viable study path** |
| --- |
| Is it possible to reduce the complexity of the curricula by grouping modules and courses into larger entities? |
| Identify the fundamental and supplemental elements of each curriculum. Which elements are absolutely mandatory, which could be treated as optional? |
| For two-year study programs on both sides: Is it possible to credit the compulsory elements from one study program as electives in the study program of the other institution and vice versa? |
| For a combination of a one-year and a two-year study program: Is it possible to credit the one-year study program as an elective in the context of the two-year study program? |
| Make sure the institutions contribute equally to the overall workload in the program. Usually this 50/50 approach best satisfies existing degree and exam regulations. |
| Is it possible to define "black boxes" for credit transfer above module level that facilitate the satisfaction of existing degree regulations? |

| **Assess potential legal and organizational barriers** |
| --- |
| Make sure that you have identified all potential barriers to your double degree program, including regulations on an institutional, state and national level. |
| Ensure that you understand the context of the regulations at your partner institution. Example: when converting ECTS credits to contact hours, take into account that the actual conversion rate is highly dependent on the proportion of self-study and group-work hours, which may differ from the conventions at your institution. |
| Try to keep the program structure as simple as possible and minimize the legal and organizational overhead required by the double degree program. The more changes you have to implement and the more resources you need, the more resistance you will face. |
| Be aware that you most likely will not be able to avoid adjusting the existing regulations at your institution. Check if you can satisfy the requirements by passing amendments to existing rules instead of creating new regulations from scratch. |

# Transatlantic Degree Program – At a Glance

| | | | | | |
|---|---|---|---|---|---|
| Name of Program | Double Master in Business Administration | | | | |
| Partner Institutions | Helsinki School of Economics<br>Louvain School of Management<br>University of Cologne | | | | |
| Location of Study | Cologne/Germany, Helsinki/Finland, Louvain/Belgium | | | | |
| Academic Field(s) | Business Administration, Management | | | | |
| Academic Level | Master | | | | |
| Year Started | 2008 | What type of degree is awarded? | | Double | |
| Language(s) of Instruction | English, German (optional), French (optional), Finnish (optional) | | | | |
| How many students participated in the most recent year of the program? | | | | | |
| | EU students | 16 | U.S. students | 0 | Other students | 1 |
| How many students have graduated from the program since it began? | | | | | |
| | EU students | 0 | U.S. students | 0 | Other students | 0 |

## The European Experience – Program Design and Implementation

# MANAGING STUDENT AND FACULTY MOBILITY

BY HILARY JONES AND CHRISTOPHER GRINBERGS

## Introduction

For the past five years, Roehampton University, London, has been the coordinating institution for the joint MA/Mgr Special Education Needs with Fontys University of Applied Sciences (The Netherlands) and Charles University (Czech Republic) and for the past three years for a multiple degree, MA Human Rights Practice, with Gothenburg University (Sweden) and Tromsø University (Norway).  Both of these programs are supported by the European Commission's Erasmus Mundus Program and involve the mobility of staff and scholars (faculty) among the three institutions involved in each program.

In this article, we seek to make practical recommendations, which consist of tried and tested current methods that have been continually evolving and developing through the life cycle of the programs.  One of the key characteristics of successful joint and multiple degree programs is that both the academic and administrative aspects of the program work together to enhance the student experience and allow for successful mobility of both students and faculty.

For the purpose of managing student and faculty mobility, we believe it is essential to investigate five key areas more thoroughly:

- Preparatory Phase
- Selection Process
- Finances
- Visas
- Accommodation

## Preparatory Phase

It is important, when working on a collaborative program, for the program to be thoroughly planned and for the partners to be aware of their responsibilities.  Because these arrangements are so crucial to the success of the program, we have incorporated them into the legally binding Memorandum of Agreement (MOA) that is reviewed annually in updated annexes. The MOA is in place for the duration of the program. Annual changes to practice and the manner in which the program is delivered, as well as any other revisions or alterations, are formally agreed upon in an annex that accompanies the MOA. This is discussed and negotiated at the Joint Program Board, where representatives of each institution discuss issues related to the program twice a year. The final details and agreements for the following year derive from the summer meeting of the Joint Program Board. The annex is then signed by all partners, indicating that all formal arrangements are set out and agreed upon by all partners.

Details to be agreed upon include the academic content of the program, a schedule of session delivery, dates for submission of coursework, and the role of each partner in administration. As mentioned previously, for these programs to work successfully it is essential that administrators and academics work closely together during the initial implementation stage. A number of considerations need to be taken into account when arranging for student mobility. The mobility pattern needs to be clear and transparent from the outset so that the consortium collaboratively, and at each partner university, is able to:

1. Put processes in place.

2. Enable students to plan their academic year in advance (e.g., arrange flights as early as possible to get the best offers available).

3. Advise students on available student services, particularly if they arrive outside normal arrangements or if academic calendars do not match.

4. Assess visa issues that many arise according to the mobility pattern.

5. Decide how finances will be arranged—will students/scholars be able to set up bank accounts? Or, if scholarships are to be received, how will they be administered and received?

6. Reserve accommodation—currently, most joint/double degrees are at the master's level, and there are not always as many possibilities for master's-level students in university accommodation.

## Selection Process

In the case of both our master's programs, processes to be put in place include the recruitment of students to the program and the selection process. From the outset, it is necessary to negotiate how the consortium would agree on different education systems—in one country, a national call goes out and students have two weeks to apply to their master's programs, in another all students are required to have face-to-face interviews with photographic identification, which means telephone interviews would not be permissible. For the purposes of these programs (predominantly non-European students) it was unrealistic and unfeasible to invite all candidates to an interview. Thus, it was necessary to establish joint selection criteria and processes so that all consortium members' criteria were met and all members shared ownership of the final student list.

Both of our consortia have a collaborative selection process involving all members, as outlined in the original bid. The deadline for entry is set in December of the year before entry. Then one academic member and two administrative members of the Roehampton staff review each application against the consortium's selection criteria, with attention given to the first/second degree and English language proficiency attained by applicants. The applications that meet these basic criteria are then circulated to representatives of all three universities, who give a mark out of 20. At a joint meeting at one of the partner institutions, the marks are entered onto a spreadsheet, which is evaluated. Using this points system, a list of students is drawn up, as is a reserve list. This list is further scrutinized by the Roehampton administrator to ensure all guidelines are met. The students are notified of the outcomes. This procedure has produced a high-caliber cohort of students.

## Finances

If the program involves scholarship delivery, detailed discussions need to take place in the consortium prior to starting the program. Discussions should address the fees to be charged and how the scholarship will be paid to students living in various countries.

Any fees should be clearly agreed upon among the consortium members, so that from the beginning, students can be advised of the amount and timing of payments and budget accordingly. Subsequently, the partners need to decide how the collected sums will be divided. In one of our consortia, one of the partners did not allow student "fees," while for the institution in the UK they were a statutory obligation, so a common criterion had to be established.

When arranging student scholarship payments, some banks will not automatically open bank accounts for foreign students who rely on scholarships to cover living expenses or who are studying for a limited time. Another problem that we faced with both programs was that in the UK, the transfer of monthly scholarships to students involved significant fees. It was therefore necessary to investigate the most cost-effective means of transferring the scholarships, which has resulted in our partner universities facilitating the student finances. Students receive payments into one bank account, which they can access in all the countries in which they will study throughout the program, so there is no need to change details or procedures each time a student moves to another institution. We needed to negotiate and write into the MOA a detailed list of our auditor's expectations and the necessary paperwork.

## Visas

In some joint and dual programs, students who are unable to follow a compulsory mobility due to visa issues have been unable to complete their programs.

Due to current political situations, some visas are more difficult to obtain than others. It is important to understand the requirements of each country involved in the program in the preparatory stages, as some visas may take three to six months to be issued. Due to the nature of some of our mobility patterns, it has been necessary to negotiate special arrangements with embassies to facilitate the movement of groups of students. Developing good relationships with contacts at the necessary embassies helps to ease the process and can lead to the speedy resolution of any issues.

Students must apply for visas as soon as possible. For both of our programs, we have pre-departure booklets that detail each country's visa requirements. Furthermore, we send a list of students to the embassies of their home countries, communicate with students to ensure the process goes smoothly, and ensure that all necessary visa documentation is sent out at the same stage.

## Accommodation

Once their visas have been arranged, students and faculty are often most concerned about where they will live. We include accommodation details in pre-departure information, so that students can see where they will live throughout their programs and are aware of budgetary needs. This information includes a short description of the available facilities, cost of living in them, and procedures for room reservation. Some students will want to bring family with them, but within our consortia it is not possible to arrange accommodation that is suitable for families. Students are warned of this and informed of alternative accommodation possibilities and associated costs, which are higher than the cost of student accommodation. Students on these programs can be informed about living accommodations and washing/kitchen facilities at an early stage, which can make mobility arrangements easier.

Accommodation needs to be identified and reserved in advance. We have to make special arrangements for our programs as our students sometimes arrive at the host campus at times that do not coincide with the start of the regular semester. This complicates efforts to ensure efficient use of each university's resources and a high standard of service to students and faculty.

## Conclusions and Recommendations

In our experience, careful planning can ensure a successful program and easy, rewarding mobility for all staff and faculty involved. To this end we recommend:

- A dedicated project manager for the program who is able to assist the academics and also the students (both incoming and outgoing).

- Clear mobility patterns explained to students at the earliest opportunity, possibly in a pre-departure handbook including details of financial, accommodation, and visa arrangements.

- Developing close relationships with all key players both within universities (accommodation office, finance, registry, international departments, etc.), within consortia (identifying key people in each of the institutions for student and staff to approach), and with external bodies (embassies, funding bodies, etc.).

- A detailed agreement between consortium members regarding responsibilities in order to ensure a truly collaborative program.

Taking a cohesive approach to the academic and administrative aspects of the program will ensure that mobility is integrated, well run, and rewarding for all students and faculty involved.

# Transatlantic Degree Program – At a Glance

| Name of Program | Erasmus Mundus MA Special Education Needs (EMSEN) | | | | |
|---|---|---|---|---|---|
| Partner Institutions | Fontys University of Applied Sciences, Tilburg, The Netherlands<br>Univerzita Karlova v Praze (Charles University), Prague, Czech Republic<br>Roehampton University, London, UK | | | | |
| Location of Study | Roehampton (2 intensive weeks), Fontys (6 months), Charles (2 intensive weeks), one of the 3 universities for dissertation 5 months | | | | |
| Academic Field(s) | Special Education Needs | | | | |
| Academic Level | Master's | | | | |
| Year Started | 2005 | What type of degree is awarded? | | Joint | |
| Language(s) of Instruction | | English (cultural Dutch and Czech) | | | |
| How many students participated in the most recent year of the program? 21 | | | | | |
| | EU students | 1 | U.S. students | 0 | Other students | 20 |
| How many students have graduated from the program since it began? | | | | | |
| | EU students | 4 | U.S. students | 0 | Other students | 125 |

| Name of Program | Erasmus Mundus Human Rights Practice | | | | |
|---|---|---|---|---|---|
| Partner Institutions | Gothenburg University, Sweden<br>Tromso Univeristy, Norway<br>Roehampton University, London, UK | | | | |
| Location of Study | Year 1: One semester Gothenburg, one semester Roehampton, Year 2: One semester Tromso and one semester at one of three locations for dissertation | | | | |
| Academic Field(s) | Human Rights Practice | | | | |
| Academic Level | Master's | | | | |
| Year Started | 2007 | What type of degree is awarded? | | Double | |
| Language(s) of Instruction | | English (cultural Norwegian and Swedish) | | | |
| How many students participated in the most recent year of the program? | | | | | |
| | EU students | 5 | U.S. students | 4 | Other students | 31 |
| How many students have graduated from the program since it began? | | | | | |
| | EU students | 4 | U.S. students | 0 | Other students | 16 |

*Appendix A*
# ABOUT THE CONTRIBUTORS

**Jürgen E. Blechschmidt** is a Professor of Mechanical Engineering at University of Applied Sciences Lübeck (FHL). Prior to joining the faculty at FHL in 1994, he spent six years in an enterprise producing self-propelled cleaning machines for the international market, ultimately as a department manager in research and development. Blechschmidt earned his Diplom-Ingenieur degree in mechanical engineering from Technical University of Clausthal, Germany, where he also received his PhD. His research was in the field of strength, engineering design, and machine component design, and his thesis concerned the endurance life of special thread geometry. Blechschmidt has published papers in the fields of threads, machine design, and engineering education. He is program director for an exchange program for mechanical engineering students (ISM) between the Milwaukee School of Engineering and FHL. He is also currently Vice-Dean of the Department of Mechanical Engineering and Business Administration at FHL. From 2003 to 2009, Blechschmidt held a guest professorship in Mechanical Engineering at Växjö Universitet, Sweden.

**Nora Bonnin** is the Associate Director of the Office of International Affairs at the University of Illinois at Chicago. Her current work focuses mainly on assisting university faculty and administrators to produce guidelines that institutionalize international educational initiatives on campuses. She has held administrative positions in international education since 1987. She has published on the impact of international education on regional development and higher education, and investigated the spread of HIV across the southern border among migrants between central Mexico and the Midwest. She is a native of Argentina and holds degrees from institutions in Argentina and the U.S. She is currently pursuing her PhD in Education.

**Jenifer Cushman** came to Juniata College in July 2007 as Dean of the Center for International Programs. She has presented research and led study abroad programs at universities in Germany, Italy, Poland, Russia, and the UK. After teaching English with the U.S. Peace Corps at a pedagogical university in Russia and then privately in Poland, Cushman accepted the position of Assistant Professor of German and Russian at the University of Minnesota, Morris (UMM), where she received tenure and promotion to Associate Professor in 2005. Cushman then served as Director of International and Off-Campus Study at the College of Wooster in Wooster, Ohio, from 2005 to 2007, and as the Ohio state representative for NAFSA Region VI in 2006-2007. She is currently President of the Midwest Modern Language Association. Cushman received a PhD in German Literature from the Ohio State University in 1996.

**Christi Degen** began her career in strategic development of internationalization at educational institutions 18 years ago when she earned her master's degree in economics. As International Relations Director at the Faculty of Management, Economics and Social Sciences (WiSo-Faculty) at the University of Cologne, she has defined the strategic objectives of internationalization for the faculty and led the implementation process. Between 1999 and 2004 she was the Programme Development Director in the Community of European Management Schools (CEMS), a network of leading management schools and multinational companies. She conceptualized and implemented the CEMS Master's of International Management, which is now offered by 23 business schools. In 2009 she joined the Rotonda Business Club as Director of the International Lounge. She develops and moderates internationally oriented events that aim to increase knowledge of internationally relevant topics in business, culture, and society.

**Pascal Delisle** is the Cultural Attaché for Higher Education at the French Embassy in Washington, DC, and founding director of the Partner University Fund, which promotes innovative partnerships in research and higher education between France and the U.S. Previously, Delisle was the director of the American Center at Sciences Po in Paris. From 2002 to 2004 he was a visiting professor at Columbia University, where he founded the Alliance Program, a strategic joint venture among Columbia University, Sciences Po, Ecole Polytechnique, and Université Paris I Panthéon-Sorbonne. Formerly, Delisle held several faculty positions in France, at Columbia University and Georgetown University, publishing articles and book chapters mostly on environmental and European economics. A native of France, Delisle holds a PhD in Environmental Economics from Université Paris I Panthéon-Sorbonne. He is a graduate of Sciences Po in Public Policy and also received a degree from Ecole Normale Supérieure.

**Anne Sheridan Fugard** is the Director of Study Abroad in the Coggin College of Business at the University of North Florida. She currently directs the student services aspect of the GlobalMBA and the newly created Ibero-American MBA. Previously, she worked in the Warrington College of Business at the University of Florida. Fugard will earn her Doctor of Education in Educational Leadership from the University of North Florida in 2009. She also earned a Master of Education in Student Personnel in Higher Education from the University of Florida and a Bachelor of Science in Elementary Education from Ohio University.

**Stephan Geifes** has been scientific coordinator of the German Historical Institute in Paris since October 2008. He was previously secretary general of the Franco-German University from 2005 to 2008, director of the Paris office of the German Academic Exchange Service (DAAD) from 2001 to 2005, and assistant to the board at DAAD headquarters in Bonn from 1999 to 2000. Geifes studied history, sociology, Romance languages, and political science at the University of Bielefeld (Germany), the Ecoles des hautes études en sciences sociales (EHESS, Paris) and at the Institut d'études politiques

(IEP, Paris). After earning a master's degree in history from the University of Bielefeld in 1996, he continued his studies from 1997 to 1999 at the master of public administration level at the Ecole nationale d'administration (ENA, Paris/Strasbourg).

**Christopher Grinbergs** works as the Bids and Erasmus Mundus Officer in the Research and Business Development Office at Roehampton University. Grinbergs helps to prepare a variety of bids and looks after the administration of the Erasmus Mundus programs. He is currently undertaking a PhD looking at the international student experience in joint programs, focusing on Erasmus Mundus. His research looks into the effect on students of studying at multiple locations and the extent to which this fosters wider international cooperation in higher education. Grinbergs pursued undergraduate studies in French at the Universities of Warwick and Grenoble and a master's degree in broadcast journalism at the University of Sheffield.

**Peter Gustavsson** is Director of Studies and Department Head for Business Administration at Linköping University in Linköping, Sweden. He is the Swedish Project Manager for the Atlantis exchange project. An internationally respected author and researcher, he is well known for his expertise in internationalization and strategy. He has lectured around the world and has developed and taught graduate and undergraduate courses on topics of power, strategy, and change management. He also supervises graduate research projects. His professional experience is in banking, and he maintains close contact with the business community through placing interns, conducting research, and advising businesses. He has authored over 30 journal articles and has coauthored five books.

**Sarah A. Hutchison** assumed the position of Academic Coordinator for the TransAtlantic Masters (TAM) Program at the University of North Carolina at Chapel Hill (UNC-CH) in the summer of 2002 while at work on her doctoral dissertation. She earned her PhD in Comparative Literature from UNC-CH in 2003. She now continues to work at UNC-CH's Center for European Studies as TAM's Associate Director. Over the past seven years, her work has focused on TAM recruitment and admissions, current student coordination, and alumni relations and development. Hutchison has taught several undergraduate courses at Carolina and has recently completed a book chapter focused on the role of foreign language skills and U.S.-based social science MA programs; the text will be part of a forthcoming work published by Mellon Press and called Languages Mean Business: Integrating Languages And Cultures in/for the Professions, edited by Professor Michel Gueldry.

**Vuokko Iinatti** is Coordinator of Studies in the Oulu Business School of the University of Oulu in Finland. Her main responsibility is international student affairs in the Oulu Business School administration. She has coordinated the double degree program between the University of Oulu and the University of North Carolina at Greensboro for the last year and a half and has acted as a contact person between the two universities and the students. She received an MS in Economics and Business Administration in 2008 from the University of Oulu.

Hilary Jones is Head of Bids, Grants and Project Innovation in the Research and Business Development Office at Roehampton University, London. Jones co-wrote and supported the bidding and validation process for the university's successful Erasmus Mundus Master's in Special Education Needs (SEN) and also Erasmus Mundus Master's in Human Rights Practice (HRP). She manages the administration across the consortia of both of the Erasmus Mundus projects. During her 11 years at Roehampton, Jones has worked in quality academic standards, the Socrates Programme and in the International Centre. Before working at Roehampton, she was Director and Company Secretary of her own travel company, following a three-year stint working in a wholesale travel company. Jones is currently researching international cooperation in education.

Carsten Klenner is a project manager at the International Relations Center of the Faculty of Economics, Management and Social Sciences at the University of Cologne. In this position he advises and supports faculty management in the strategic development of the faculty's international cooperation activities. His tasks include the initiation, conceptual development, and implementation of pioneering international cooperation activities – including the Cologne double master program, the European research platform EZMF, and the Sino-German cooperation network China-NRW. Klenner is a permanent member of the research group "Information Systems and Learning Processes (ISLP)" at the University of Cologne and a guest researcher at the research group MI²EO at the University of Koblenz-Landau. His research interests include change management and implementation of information systems in organizations. Before holding a job at the University of Cologne he worked in the IT industry and as a consultant. He holds a degree in information systems.

Ulla Kriebernegg studied English and American Studies and German Philology at Karl-Franzens University Graz, Austria, and at University College Dublin, Ireland. She was also a Visiting Scholar at the Boston College Center for International Higher Education (CIHE) and Montclair State University, NJ. From 1999 to 2007, she worked for Graz University's Office of International Relations, where she was centrally involved in joint degree development. She now works as an Assistant Professor for the Center of the Study of the Americas at Karl-Franzens University Graz. Her doctoral research, "Transatlantic Relationships in Higher Education: An Analysis of Cultural Narratives," explores the impact of the Bologna reforms on U.S. higher education. Her research interests are inter-American studies, interculturality, and U.S. and European higher education policy. Kriebernegg holds a master's degree in English and American studies and German philology.

Matthias Kuder works as program manager with the Center for International Cooperation, a new strategic unit promoting internationalization at Freie Universität Berlin, Germany. He served as project manager and junior officer with the Embassy of Canada and with the Canadian Universities' Centre, a liaison office of Canadian universities in Berlin. Kuder also worked as consultant with Lemmens Media, a German agency specializing in consulting services for higher education institutions and research organizations. Prior to joining the Center for International Cooperation, he coordinated the Transatlantic Degree Programs (TDP) Project at Freie Universität as well as the development of an international PhD program on Ethics and Human Rights. Kuder studied in Bonn, Toronto, and Berlin and holds a master's degree in North American Studies and Political Science from Freie Universität.

**Régine Lambrech** began her tenure as Director of Global Initiatives and Education at Columbia University's Fu Foundation School of Engineering and Applied Sciences in January of 2009. She is the author of numerous publications in the field of international education and has been active in the field as a consultant specializing in study abroad program development, crisis management for study abroad, and risk analysis and risk management for international programs. Before joining Columbia University, Lambrech was Director of International Relations at the Ecole Centrale de Lyon in France, where she was instrumental in the development of dual degree programs. She received her PhD in French from the Pennsylvania State University.

**Allan W. Lerner** is Associate Provost and Executive Director of the Office of International Affairs at the University of Illinois at Chicago (UIC), serving as UIC's Senior International Officer. He holds the academic positions of Professor of Public Administration and Professor of Political Science. His previous administrative positions at UIC included Associate Provost for External Education, Deputy Associate Chancellor, Interim Dean of the College of Urban Planning and Public Affairs, Associate Dean of the Graduate College, and Director of the Graduate Program in Public Administration. His published works have addressed issues in organizational adaptation, performance, and reliability in the public sector, including organizational decision processes and their interpersonal dynamics, forces affecting the recovery from catastrophe, organizational learning, and strategic organizational innovation.

**Roberta Maierhofer** is Professor at the Department of American Studies of the University of Graz, Austria, and Adjunct Professor at Binghamton University, New York. Since joining the staff of the Department of American Studies in 1998, she has focused on developing the university's international study, joint-study, and exchange programs as well as its Office for International Relations. She was elected Vice Rector for International Relations in 1999 and then appointed for another period as Vice Rector for International Relations and Affirmative Action for Women within the new Austrian University Act in 2003. Since 2004, she has been Vice Rector for International Relations and Interdisciplinary Cooperation, and since 2007 she has served as academic director of the newly founded Center for the Study of the Americas of the University of Graz. Her research focuses on American literature and cultural studies, feminist literature and research, transatlantic cooperation in education, and aging studies. Maierhofer holds a master's and a doctoral degree from the University of Graz, as well as an MA degree in comparative literature from SUNY Binghamton.

**Tuija Mainela** started as Assistant Professor of Marketing at the Oulu Business School of the University of Oulu (Finland) in August 2002 after receiving a DSc in Marketing from the University of Vaasa. She been a professor of international business and currently has a full-time research post. She has researched and published articles on the dynamics of business networks, international entrepreneurship, the development of teaching in a foreign language, and social relationships and value creation in business networks. Mainela has developed and taught undergraduate and graduate courses on topics in marketing and international business. She studied as a master-level exchange student at the University of Umeå, Sweden, and completed the European Doctoral Program in Entrepreneurship and Small Business Management in Barcelona, Spain, and Växjö, Sweden.

**Jeffrey Michelman** is a professor of accounting and Co-Director of the Flagship Program in International Business at the University of North Florida. Michelman has published articles in journals of information systems, accounting, international business, and healthcare. He has written three textbooks and developed several computer software programs to integrate technology into the accounting curriculum. Michelman has taught in France, China, Poland, and Fiji and is currently a Visiting Professor at Warsaw University. He has been a member of several visiting committees of the Commission for Academic Accreditation, Ministry of Higher Education and Scientific Research, United Arab Emirates.

**Kathleen E. Murphy** is currently a full professor at Daemen College in Amherst, New York, where she has also served as both chair of the Division of Natural and Health Sciences and departmental chair for natural sciences. Her main research interests involve projects in environmental chemistry, case studies on the interplay of science and politics in local environmental problems, and developing hydrogels as delivery mechanisms for the treatment of chronic wounds. From 2004 to 2009, she was the U.S. project director for an EU-FIPSE grant in the EU-U.S. Atlantis Program involving three U.S. and three European colleges. The program developed a model for a one-semester international exchange of science students, with students combining coursework in traditional areas of science with the study of applications of biotechnology to chronic wounds. She received a PhD in Physical Chemistry from the University of Vermont and completed postdoctoral research in polymer chemistry at Rensselaer Polytechnic Institute.

**Joseph C. Musto** is a professor in the Mechanical Engineering Department at Milwaukee School of Engineering, where he teaches in the areas of machine design, solid modeling, and numerical methods. Prior to joining the faculty at Milwaukee School of Engineering, he held industrial positions with Brady Corporation and Eastman Kodak Company, and he is a registered Professional Engineer in Wisconsin. He holds a BS degree from Clarkson University in Potsdam, New York, and both an MEng and a PhD from Rensselaer Polytechnic Institute, all in mechanical engineering.

**Eleanor (El) Nault** has served at the Director of Assessment at Clemson University for over a decade. Her commitment to institutional effectiveness underpins her work as a researcher, faculty member, and author. Both national and international works have been the hallmarks of her NSF, FIPSE, and Howard Hughes grant assessment projects as an independent evaluator. Additionally, she serves on professional boards and is qualified as a site visitor for higher education institutional reaffirmation by the Southern Association of Colleges and Schools Commission on Colleges. To complement her academic work, Nault is dedicated to general service projects at the local and national levels. She is a native of South Carolina and received a PhD in educational leadership from Clemson University.

**Jerome L. Neuner** is Associate Vice President for Academic Affairs at Canisius College. His academic background is in text linguistics and the teaching of writing. His administrative responsibilities include the offices of faculty development, sponsored programs, graduate fellowships, and special events, as well as international partnerships and exchanges. His work has been supported by the National Endowment for the Humanities, the U.S. Department of Education, the New York State Department of Education, as well as several national private foundations. He has delivered conference papers at international events. He earned his PhD from the Graduate School of Education at the State University of New York at Buffalo.

**Daniel Obst** is Director of Membership and Higher Education Services at the Institute of International Education (IIE) in New York. He directs all the activities of the Institute's university membership association of over 1,000 higher education institutions around the world and oversees IIE's print and online publications. He is also editor of *IIENetworker*, IIE's international education magazine, and the executive editor of IIE's Global Education Research Reports, which focus on key issues in international higher education. Obst recently completed a survey on transatlantic joint and dual/double degree programs for the EU-U.S. Atlantis Program. He is also responsible for all of IIE's conferences, seminars, and workshops and is a frequent presenter at conferences and workshops, focusing especially on transatlantic academic exchange. Obst, who was born and raised in Germany, received his BA in international relations from the George Washington University and holds an MA in European studies from the London School of Economics.

**John E. Pakkala** is an associate professor of mechanical engineering at Milwaukee School of Engineering (MSOE). Before coming to MSOE in 2001, he spent more than 20 years as a special machine designer and was involved with the design, construction, and installation of machines and manufacturing automation equipment for automotive, aerospace, and defense industry clients. Pakkala earned a BS in mechanical engineering from Michigan State University. His MS and PhD degrees in electrical engineering from Michigan Technological University were in the area of dynamic control theory and system identification. He has published papers in fluid mechanics, internal combustion engine controls, system identification, and engineering education. He is currently the director of an exchange program for mechanical engineering students between MSOE and the Fachhochschule Lübeck in Lübeck, Germany.

**Hans H. Reddemann** is a professor of mechanical engineering at University of Applied Sciences Lübeck (FHL). Before coming to FHL in 1995, he spent more than seven years as a project leader in aviation industry. He was involved in the design and development, construction and installation, manufacturing and testing of life support and protective systems in civil and military aviation projects. Reddemann earned his Diplom-Ingenieur degree in mechanical engineering from Technical University of Braunschweig, Germany. His PhD in mechanical engineering from Technical University of Braunschweig was in the area of analysis and simulation of electro-mechanical vibrations of centrifugal systems. He has published papers in vibration control and engineering education. He initiated, introduced, and is still in charge of an exchange program for mechanical engineering students from the Milwaukee School of Engineering and FHL. He is also currently Dean of the Department of Mechanical Engineering and Business Administration at FHL.

**Macarena Sáez** is the International Programs Coordinator for the American University Washington College of Law (WCL). Sáez directs the International JD Dual Degree Programs at WCL that offers dual law degrees with the Universities of Paris X-Nanterre, France; Monash University Law School, Australia; University of Ottawa Faculty of Law, Canada; and the University Carlos III Law School, Spain. Additionally, she teaches the "Introduction to the Continental Legal System" course at WCL. Prior to joining WCL, she taught jurisprudence and feminist legal theory at the University of Chile. Sáez holds a Licenciada en Derecho (JD equivalent) from the University of Chile School of Law and an LLM from Yale Law School.

**Emeric Solymossy** is an entrepreneur, executive manager, and Fulbright-Hall Distinguished Chair for Entrepreneurship in Central Europe (2008-2009). He travels extensively and thrives on international collaboration and foreign opportunities. He is a professor at Western Illinois University in the Quad Cities, teaching business management and research methods, and specializes in entrepreneurship, leadership, and strategic planning. His research explores the factors that influence entrepreneurial success. His interests are international, which is reflected in his frequent collaboration and international consulting. He is currently investigating the nature of knowledge networks and how knowledge is valued within the organization as well as in the marketplace. He has published extensively, and his work appears in five languages. He is on the editorial board for the *International Entrepreneurship and Management Journal*, a reviewer for two other journals as well as four textbook publishers, and has received numerous awards for his research and teaching.

**Jeffrey W. Steagall** is Richard deRaismes Kip Professor of International Business at the University of North Florida, where he has been a leader in internationalizing the Coggin College of Business. He led its first study abroad course in 1998 and has arranged 20 student exchange programs with foreign universities. Steagall helped design the majors in international business (IB) and international studies, the graduate concentration and certificate in IB, and the GlobalMBA, as well as the new Ibero-American MBA program, an international double-degree program requiring students to study in two languages. He has published numerous articles on international business education and study abroad.

**Lori Thompson** is Associate Director for International Partnerships in the Office of International Programs at the State University of New York (SUNY) System Administration, located in Albany, New York. Thompson worked extensively on development of the system's programs with Turkish universities from their inception soon after she arrived at SUNY in 2000. In 2004, she established the SUNY office in Ankara, Turkey, where she remained as director until returning to Albany in 2008. The office manages the system-wide program and coordinates communication among SUNY and its Turkish university partners, the Turkish Higher Education Council, the U.S. Embassy and Consulates, and other government offices. As director, Thompson was responsible for overseeing program promotion and visa procurement, among other duties. She now works primarily on program development in the Near East and Asia. Thompson received a BA in English writing from St. Lawrence University.

**Paul Tomkins** is currently head of the faculty of science in Athlone Institute of Technology in Ireland. Tomkins is a toxicologist who in the past decade launched a spin-out company, Bioserv Ltd, and a research facility, the Centre for Biopolymer & Biomolecular Research. His research priorities are in cell line development and cell and molecular toxicology, with applications to novel mechanistic and high throughput screening assays. Tomkins has collaborated with partner institutions in France, Italy, Finland, UK, Switzerland, Germany, Israel, and the U.S., in the context of research and joint education. His group also provides process and IP support for industry in the biomedical sector. Recently, Tomkins was the European coordinator of an EU-FIPSE international student exchange project under the EU-U.S. Atlantis program. He completed his PhD at the National University of Ireland Galway and has undertaken seconded research in Canada and Australia.

**Jamie Welling** is the International Programs Analyst for the American University Washington College of Law (WCL). She works mainly on the International JD Dual Degree Program, which partners with schools in Canada, France, Spain, and Australia, and on developing strategic partnerships for the law school. Prior to joining WCL, Welling worked for various domestic and international nongovernmental organizations focusing on issues such as international economic development and legal policy, grant administration, and the Middle East. Jamie holds a Master of Public Administration in International Management from the American University School of Public Affairs.

*Appendix B*
# ABOUT THE EU-U.S. ATLANTIS PROGRAM

The European Union-United States Atlantis Program is a grant competition conducted cooperatively by the U.S. Department of Education's Fund for the Improvement of Postsecondary Education (FIPSE) and the European Commission's Directorate General for Education and Culture (DG EAC). It provides grants for up to four years to add a European Community-United States dimension to international curriculum development and related student exchange.

The purpose of this competition is to promote a student-centered, transatlantic dimension to higher education and training in a wide range of academic and professional disciplines. The Atlantis Program will fund collaborative efforts to develop programs of study leading to joint or dual undergraduate or graduate degrees. The program will also fund a small number of policy-oriented grants and one-team mobility grants.

More information is available at:
www.ed.gov/programs/fipseec/index.html
http://ec.europa.eu/education/programmes/eu-usa/index_en.html

## ATLANTIS GRANT AWARDS – FY 2008

The following section contains program names, summaries and contact information for projects that received grants from the EU-U.S. Atlantis Program in FY 2008.

For awards from previous Atlantis grant years, please visit:
www.ed.gov/programs/fipseec/awards.html.

## Mobility Project in Integral Valorization of Bioproduction

U.S. Lead:   University of Arkansas
             Iowa State University
             Kansas State University

EU Lead:   University of Ghent (Belgium)
           Karl Franzens University at Graz (Austria)
           Toulouse Polytechnic University (France)

This mobility project will develop an innovative program to bridge the gap in traditional teaching programs for agriculture and food science as well as those in renewable resources and biomaterials. Students will study agricultural resources as they relate to the food production chain and the effective use of renewable co-products.

CONTACTS:   Andrew Proctor, University of Arkansas, proctor@uark.edu
            Dewettinck Koen, Ghent University, koen.dewettinck@ugent.be


## Undergraduate Dual Degree Program in International Relations

U.S. Lead:   Grand Valley State University (Michigan)

EU Lead:   Cracow University of Economics (Poland)
           University of Debrecen (Hungary)

This undergraduate dual degree program focuses on the study of international relations. The project will focus on economics, political theory, and public policy issues in Europe and the US for students earning degrees in international relations. The project also includes development of a shared course and faculty teaching residencies.

CONTACTS:   Mark Schaub, Grand Valley State University, schaubm@gvsu.edu
            Patkaniowski Michał, Cracow University of Economics,
               michal.patkaniowski@uek.krakow.pl


## Undergraduate Dual Degree Program in Hotel Management

U.S. Lead:   Oklahoma State University

EU Lead:   Robert Gordon University (United Kingdom)
           Turku University of Applied Science (Finland)

This dual degree undergraduate program in hotel management aims to train transatlantic hotel managers. The students involved in this program will follow a flexible pathway through three undergraduate degree programs across the three universities with a focus on the international context of decision making and the cultural dimension of planning in international hospitality.

CONTACTS:   Radesh Palakurthi, Oklahoma State University, palakur@okstate.edu
            Richard Barnes, Robert Gordon University, r.barnes@rgu.ac.uk


## Graduate Dual Degree Program in Forest Resources

U.S. Lead:   North Carolina State University
             Michigan Technological University

EU Lead:   Swedish University of Agricultural Sciences (Sweden)
           University of Helsinki (Finland)

The overall objectives of the EU-U.S. Transatlantic Masters Degree Program in Forest Resources are to educate graduate students in forest resources management, to enhance global competitiveness of forestry in the temperate climatic zone, to contribute to sustainable management of forests globally, and to enhance teaching practices and the quality of higher education in forestry in the EU and the U.S.

CONTACTS:  Bronson Bullock, NC State University, sps@ncsu.edu
Matts Lindbladh, Swedish University of Agricultural Sciences,
    matts.lindbladh@ess.slu.se

## Undergraduate Dual Degree Program in Paper Science and Engineering

U.S. Lead:  University of Wisconsin-Stevens Point
North Carolina State University

EU Lead:  University of Applied Sciences – München (Germany)
Tampere Polytechnic University of Applied Sciences (Finland)
Jyvasklia University of Applied Sciences (Finland)

The project goal is to implement a Transatlantic Paper Science (TAPS) dual undergraduate degree to study global paper science through international collaboration. Today's professionals need to have a strong scientific background and understand industry-related environmental challenges in this global enterprise. TAPS has four components: vocational/academic exchange, intensive language training, online discussion forum, and a work internship in model paper science industry.

CONTACTS:  Bobbi Kubish, University of Wisconsin, Stevens Point,
    Bobbi.Kubish@uwsp.edu
Stephan Kleeman and Annabelle Wolff, University of Applied Sciences -
    München, kleemann@hm.edu; wolff1@hm.edu

## Mobility Project in Micro- and Nano-systems

U.S. Lead:  University of Arizona
New Mexico State University

EU Lead:  Budapest University of Technology and Economics (Hungary)
Slovak Technical University Bratislava (Slovak Republic)

This program is an international student-training program in the area of mechanics of micro- and nano-systems. This program includes four institutions and is available to graduate and undergraduate students at each site, providing a cohort experience for the students and leading to the awarding of a certificate.

CONTACTS:  Eniko T. Enikov, University of Arizona, enikov@engr.arizona.edu
Gábor Stépán, Budapest University of Technology and Economics,
    stepan@mm.bme.hu

## Mobility Project in Urban Studies

U.S. Lead:  University of Denver (Colorado)
Portland State University (Oregon)

EU Lead:  University of Bologna (Italy)
University of Nottingham (United Kingdom)

The project will create a joint curriculum between partner institutions focused on promoting greater awareness of the social and ecological challenges confronting contemporary cities in a time of rapid expansion in urbanization and escalating concerns about the sustainability of urban life. The program involves the exchange of students between the partner institutions to apply methodologies to urban problems.

CONTACTS: Dean Saitta, University of Denver, dsaitta@du.edu
Giovanna Franci, University of Bologna, Giovanna.franci@unibo.it

## Mobility Project in Developmental Education

U.S. Lead: University of North Carolina at Chapel Hill
Vanderbilt University (Tennessee)

EU Lead: Jonkoping University (Sweden)
Ludwig-Maximillian University, Munich (Germany)
University of Porto (Portugal)

This project on Global Education and Development Studies (GEDS) integrates student experiences at home and a semester abroad to prepare future leaders for leadership roles in education and intervention for young children. The GEDS concentration will utilize the ECI-NET website and the international curriculum to be integrated with field experience to create a training model focused on acquisition of knowledge and skills related to education policy, evaluation, and research in the US and EU.

CONTACTS: Rune Simeonsson, UNC Chapel Hill, jsimeon@email.unc.edu
Eva Björck-Åkesson, Jönköping University, eva.bjorck-akesson@hlk.hj.se

## Graduate Dual Degree Project in Transnational Law

U.S. Lead: Washington University (Missouri)

EU Lead: Universiteit Utrecht (the Netherlands)
Universita degli Studi di Trento (Italy)

The program implements a dual masters plan in transnational law with a focus on the practice of law between European nations and the United States. The study abroad includes curriculum that trains students to be adept at resolving cases involving various legal systems that cross international boundaries. At the conclusion of the program graduates would be eligible to practice law or provide legal advice in both the EU and the US.

CONTACTS: Michael Peil, Washington University, mpeil@wulaw.wustl.edu
Berrocal Vargas, Utrecht University, b.berrocal@law.uu.nl

## Policy Project in Short-Cycle Higher Education

U.S. Lead: University of Toledo (Ohio)
Owens Community College (Ohio)

EU Lead: International University College (Bulgaria)
LEIDO (the Netherlands)

The project will hold discussions and exchanges of best practices in three critical areas concerning higher education programs that focus closely on preparation for the workforce: recognition and quality assurance, links with industry, and role in life-long learning systems. The project's goal is to provide a forum for international exchange of ideas through three international conferences. The project participants will conduct a feasibility study on transatlantic collaboration in the development of degrees that fall between high secondary and full bachelors degrees.

CONTACTS:  Snejana Slantcheva-Durst, University of Toledo,
snejana.slantchevadurst@utoledo.edu
Bozhidar Bozhkov, International University College,
bozhidar.bozhkov@vumk.eu

## Mobility Project in Software Engineering

U.S. Lead:  Embry-Riddle Aeronautical University (Florida)
University of Central Florida (Florida)
University of Arizona

EU Lead:  AGH University of Science and Technology (Poland)
Brno University of Technology (Czech Republic)
Universite Joseph Fourier (France)

This mobility project is dedicated to educating engineers engaged in the development of dependable, software intensive systems in global international settings. The objective is to assure mobility exchange of graduate/master level engineering students. This program contains three facets of added value: areas of concentration not available at the home institution, opportunity for overseas research, and cultural understanding of a second country.

CONTACTS:  Andrew Kornecki, Embry-Riddle University, kornecka@erau.edu
Wojciech Grega, AGH University of Science and Technology,
wgr@ia.agh.edu.pl

## Policy Project on Entrepreneurship Education

U.S. Lead:  North Carolina State University
Brown University (Rhode Island)

EU Lead:  Loughborough University (United Kingdom)
COTEC (Portugal)

This project, known as TECnet (Technology Entrepreneurship & Commercialization network), will create a network of collaborative Web-based resources that will focus on the methods of teaching students how to create technology-based high growth ventures. The process-based curriculum will be derived from a study of the relevant literature and long-term experimentation and successful practice. TECnet will enable collaborative research on the outcomes of process-based technology entrepreneurship education and disseminate the results broadly to advance the field and, over the long term, impact the creation of high growth start-ups.

CONTACTS:  Ted Baker, NC State University, ted_baker@ncsu.edu
Regina Frank, Loughborough University, R.Frank@lboro.ac.uk

## Graduate Dual Degree Program in Laser Technology Engineering

U.S. Lead:  University of Central Florida
Clemson University (South Carolina)

EU Lead:  University of Bordeaux (France)
Freidrich Schiller University (Germany)

This graduate dual degree program is designed to specifically train manpower for the global photonics economy. The program is comprised of a two-year degree that includes materials science and laser material processing. The students will also participate in an internship. The partner institutions already have a joint doctoral program and this project is seen as preparing students for that degree. Language training and cultural courses will also be included for the students.

CONTACTS:  Martin Richardson, University of Central Florida, mcr@creol.ucf.edu
Laurent Sarger, Université Bordeaux 1, l.sarger@cpmoh.u-bordeaux1.fr

## Graduate Dual Degree Program in Agricultural Economics

U.S. Lead:  University of Arkansas
University of Florida

EU Lead:  University of Ghent (Belgium)
Humboldt University (Germany)

This project will develop and implement an international double master degree program in rural development and agricultural economics among the participants. It will train specialists with comparative knowledge on EU, US and international agricultural and rural development policies. It combines a study abroad year, case study or internship experience, language training, and cultural exposure activities.

CONTACTS:  Lucas Parsch, University of Arkansas, lparsch@uark.edu
Guido Van Huylenbroeck, Ghent University,
guido.vanhuylenbroeck@UGent.be

## Mobility Project in Small and Medium Enterprises and Entrepreneurship Education

U.S. Lead:  Clemson University (South Carolina)
University of North Florida
Appalachian State University (North Carolina)

EU Lead:  Otto-Friedrich Universitat (Germany)
Universite Catholique de Louvain (Belgium)
Universidad de Alicante (Spain)

This project focuses on the creation and operation of small and medium-size enterprises. This project will include student mobility and enhanced student support services. These improvements are designed to address issues in pre-departure orientations and student integration into the host cultures. The project helps to promote exchange students participation in the process of developing new "born global" enterprises.

CONTACTS:  Mark McKnew, Clemson University, mamckn@clemson.edu
Dodo Zu Knyphausen-Aufsess, University of Bamberg,
dodo.knyphausen@uni-bamberg.de

## Undergraduate Dual Degree Program in Information Systems

US Lead:  University of Massachusetts Boston
University of Massachusetts Dartmouth

EU Lead:  Kemi-Tornio University of Applied Sciences (Finland)
Fachhochschule Frankfurt (Germany)

This undergraduate dual degree program in information systems encompasses four universities in an effort to bring together a cohort of 24 students each year in a shared program of study including one semester at each of the four universities participating. After successfully completing the program and the degree requirements of the home institution, students will receive a bachelor's degree from both their home and one host university.

CONTACTS:    William Koehler, University of Massachusetts Boston,
             William.Koehler@umb.edu
             Leena Alalääkkölä, Kemi-Tomio University of Applied Sciences,
             leena.alalaakkola@tokem.fi

*Appendix C*
# INFORMATION AND RESOURCES

### TRANSATLANTIC DEGREE PROGRAMS (TDP) PROJECT
The Transatlantic Degree Programs (TDP) Project, hosted by Freie Universität Berlin, aims at promoting dialogue on innovative forms of cooperation and exchange between higher education institutions in North America and Europe. The TDP Project focuses on examining current trends and future potential for international collaborative degree programs and other forms of structured cross-border cooperation.

WEBSITE:   www.tdp-project.de

### IIE RESOURCES FOR STUDY ABROAD
IIE offers a single point of entry to access valuable study abroad information, including policy research, data on study abroad trends, news coverage of new developments, fact sheets for students, and dates and deadlines for major scholarship and fellowship programs.

WEBSITE:   www.iie.org/studyabroad

### IIE RESOURCES ON INTERNATIONALIZING THE CAMPUS
IIE administers a wealth of programs and provides a variety of services and resources to help U.S. colleges and universities develop and implement their strategies for greater campus internationalization.

WEBSITE:   www.iie.org/internationalizing

### OPEN DOORS REPORT ON INTERNATIONAL EDUCATIONAL EXCHANGE
The *Open Doors Report on International Educational Exchange*, supported by the U.S. Department of State, Bureau of Educational and Cultural Affairs, provides a long-standing, comprehensive statistical analysis of academic mobility between the United States and other nations.

WEBSITE:   www.opendoors.iienetwork.org

## Funding for Joint and Double Degree Programming

### EU-U.S. ATLANTIS PROGRAM
WEBSITE:   www.ed.gov/programs/fipseec/index.html
WEBSITE:   http://ec.europa.eu/education/programmes/eu-usa/index_en.html

### EU-CANADA COOPERATION PROGRAM IN HIGHER EDUCATION
WEBSITE:   http://ec.europa.eu/education/programmes/eu-canada/index_en.html

### ERASMUS MUNDUS ACTION 3: PARTNERSHIPS WITH NON-EU COUNTRIES
WEBSITE:   http://eu.daad.de/eu/erasmus/05332.html